Corrective Reading

Decoding Strategies

Enrichment Blackline Masters   **Decoding B1**

Siegfried Engelmann • *Gary Johnson*

SRA McGraw-Hill

Columbus, Ohio

A Division of The McGraw-Hill Companies

SRA/McGraw-Hill

A Division of The **McGraw·Hill** *Companies*

Printed in the United States of America.

Send all inquiries to:
SRA/McGraw-Hill
4400 Easton Commons
Columbus, OH 43219

ISBN 0-02-674783-9

8 9 10 11 12 MAL 10 09 08 07

Table of Contents

Lesson	Page	Lesson	Page

Corrective Reading
Decoding B1
Enrichment Blackline Masters

Note to the Teacher

The activities in this book reinforce the skills taught in the 1999 edition of the *Corrective Reading Decoding B1* program. Each activity provides practice in an essential reading skill, such as:

- recognition of sounds and sound combinations
- word identification
- correct spelling of words
- spelling of words with endings, such as **s, ed, ing, er, ly,** and **en**
- spelling of root words without those endings
- writing compound and other two-part words
- writing sentences
- answering comprehension questions about story passages
- demonstrating comprehension of details in stories
- sequencing activities in a story
- identifying main characters
- building oral reading fluency

(Skills are identified at the bottom of each page.)

The materials are designed to be completed as study-time homework assignments. The students are not to use the Student Book when completing the blackline master. (The *Decoding B1* Student Book and Workbook should usually remain at school.) The Blackline Master pages correspond by lesson number to the *Decoding B1* lesson numbers. The Blackline Masters should be assigned as homework on the <u>same day</u> that the corresponding lesson is <u>completed</u> at school.

Students should be able to complete the homework assignments without any special instructions from the teacher or from a parent. In Lessons 1 and 2, a note to the parent at the bottom of the page directs the parent to ask the student what sound should be circled in the first row of letters and what word should be circled in the second row. All other exercises can be completed without additional instructions.

Timed Reading

To provide additional practice in building oral reading fluency, someone at home can listen to the student read aloud. These timed readings begin at Lesson 12. The procedure is similar to that of the regular program timed readings, which begin at Lesson 12. The passage that appears in the second page of the Blackline Master for Lessons 12 through 65 is taken from the first part of the story from the previous lesson. For Lesson 12, students read part of the story from Lesson 11 at home, and so forth. The student reads aloud for one minute to a parent or listener who follows along and signals when the student is to stop. The number of words read in one minute and the number of errors are recorded, and the parent/listener signs at the bottom of the page. The student brings the signed page to school on the next school day as part of the daily two-page homework assignment.

Checking Homework

The homework should be checked each day. The most efficient procedure is to conduct a teacher-directed group workcheck. Students exchange homework papers. The teacher reads the correct answers aloud as the students mark each other's papers.

- For each activity, identify the part number, then read the answers from the annotated answer key that begins on page 120 of this book.
- For exercises that require the writing of whole words or word parts, spell the words as they should appear in the answers.
- For comprehension items, read each question and say the correct answer.
- For the activities in which students fill in the missing words in a passage, read the passage aloud and say the word that should appear in the blank.
- For some activities, you can call on students to read the item and say the answer.

Homework Chart

Keep a record of the completed homework assignments. A sample Homework Chart appears on page viii. Or you may elect to use the chart that appears in *Decoding B1* instead. Points earned can be recorded in the bonus box for the regular lesson. Points could be awarded as follows:

Completing homework	2 points
0 errors	2 points
1 or 2 errors	1 point
More than 2 errors	0 points

When the timed readings begin at Lesson 12:

Completing the homework reading checkout	2 points

Point System

If you award points for homework assignments, you will need to modify the number of points required in the regular program to earn various letter grades. (For a discussion of the points and letter grades, see the discussion under "The Management System" in the *Decoding B1 Teacher's Guide*.) An alternative procedure would be to make the points earned for homework assignments separate from those earned in the regular program and to provide special incentives for completing homework.

The Blackline Master homework pages are designed so that students can be successful. Once students learn that they can complete homework successfully, they will be motivated to continue to do so. If the teacher provides positive verbal feedback for completing homework assignments, along with the use of points, students will be encouraged to do well, and their reading performance will continue to improve.

Letter to Parents

A letter explaining the general procedures for homework assignments appears on the following page. This letter should be sent home along with the first homework assignment.

Dear Parents,

Students are expected to complete homework as part of their reading lessons. The homework activities provide practice on important reading skills. In the daily homework exercises, students receive practice in the following reading skills:

- identifying the sounds of single letters and the sounds of letter combinations
- identifying words
- spelling words with endings and words without endings
- writing sentences
- answering questions about story passages
- building oral reading fluency

For Lessons 1 through 11, students complete one page of homework exercises for each lesson. Starting at Lesson 12, the homework consists of two pages. On the second page is a story passage that the student is to read aloud to someone at home. This activity provides practice on speed and accuracy.

You will need a digital watch, a digital timer (such as a kitchen timer), or a clock with a sweep second hand so that you can time the student for exactly one minute. The student starts at the first word of the passage and reads for one minute. You count the mistakes the student makes. The goal is for the student to read exactly what is on the page.

Here are the kinds of errors to count:

- saying the wrong word or mispronouncing a word
- adding a word
- leaving out a word
- adding an ending to a word (for example, reading "plays" for *play*)
- leaving off an ending (for example, reading "start" for *started*)
- not stopping at the end of a sentence
- rereading part of a sentence

At the end of one minute, stop the student. At the bottom of the page, write the number of words read in one minute and the number of errors.

If the student wants to read the passage again, write the number of times the passage was read in the blank at the bottom of the page.

Sign at the bottom of the page. The student should return the two-page homework assignment to school on the next school day.

Remember to be patient. Students who try hard need to know that they are improving. Your assistance each day will help the student improve. The more practice the student receives, the faster the student will become a better reader.

Thank you.

Corrective Reading
Decoding B1 Homework Chart

Teacher _____

Group _____

Student	Date																									
	Lesson Number																									

Part 1
Match the words.

feeds —————————•	•————————— plan
plan —————————•	•————————— man
man —————————•	•————————— lid
cat —————————•	•————————— feeds
lid —————————•	•————————— cat

Part 2

Ⓢ o e s t p l m n a a w e r s p k u b s w q a z d r t y u n b g t y u p l m n a z s d e w q s l

Ⓕⓛⓐⓣ t a o q a s f l a t m f f r t y u p l l a f l a t q e r t s v b l a t f l a t d o c x e a f l a t s e l

Part 3
Copy the sentences:

Is a man as fast as a cat?

_____

Can the cat sleep in a lap?

_____

Fill this flat pan.

_____

Matching words and letters, copying sentences
Directions, part 2: Ask the student, "What sound will you circle in the first row?" (sss) "What word will you circle in the
second row?" (flat)

Part 1

Match the words.

lamp •   • seem

feeds •   • stick

seem •   • clap

stick •   • lamp

clap •   • feeds

Part 2

(i)   e l j a i o a t r f i s d e i r c b p l i t e a g h h n m a l i o m n b g r e i j l i d e a l t

(sit)   s e l f i t s i t h a t s i t i n f i t s i s i t t i s e t s i f e f i g m i s s a t i s i t i f t i p

(this)   h i t t h e h i m i n t h i s i t i s t e e t h i f t h i s t h a t p i t d i d t h i s i n i s i t f

Part 3

Copy the sentences.

Dad can see the cats sleep.

_____

Plant this seed in the sand.

_____

Did the lamp seem dim?

_____

That cat sleeps in a tree.

_____

Matching words and letters, copying sentences
Directions, part 2: Ask the student, "What sound will you circle in the first row?" (iii) "What word will you circle in the second row?" (sit) "What word will you circle in the third row?" (this)

Name _____

Part 1

Copy the sentences:

If she is sick, I will go to the drug store.

_____

Last week, we had fun at the track meet.

_____

That truck can go as fast as a deer.

_____

Part 2

Read the sentences in the box.   Write the first word of these sentences:

| 1. Last week, we had fun at the track meet. |
| 2. Is that street as slick as it seems? |
| 3. This is the last store we will go to. |

2nd sentence _____

1st sentence _____

3rd sentence _____

Part 3

Match the words.

math   wish

needs   teeth

wish   math

drink   needs

teeth   drink

Writing sentences, writing words, matching words

LESSON 4

Name _____

Part 1

(ch) d e f a c l p o e c h s e a s h m n j s a c h e i p l t h n z s l c h f d s h f e c r q w x o s

(flag) d w f l a g e r o p l e g c z d a f l a g j h e r c l a m c I p e f l a g s a t e f l a t v b s p l a n

Part 2

Copy the sentences:

Will that milk last for a week?

_____

I need to keep that pack for the trip.

_____

Fill the gas tank in that green truck.

_____

Part 3

Match the words and complete them.

truck   sh

sheep   mi

milk   ant

drink   ink

plant   tru

Matching words and letters, copying sentences, writing words
Directions, part 1: Ask the student, "What sound will you circle in the first row?" (ch) "What word will you circle in the second row?" (flag)

Part 1

Match the words and complete them.

_____ steep	•	•	ink _____
_____ flag	•	•	ore _____
_____ drink	•	•	fl _____
_____ truck	•	•	st _____
_____ store	•	•	uck _____

Part 2

Copy the sentences:

We have a plan for a fun trip.

_____

She sat with Pam at the track meet.

_____

His clock did not run.

_____

Part 3

Read the sentences in the box.

Write the first word of these sentences:

> **1.** Fill that gold cup with milk.
>
> **2.** That truck had a flat.
>
> **3.** She did not sit with us.

3rd sentence _____

1st sentence _____

2nd sentence _____

Writing words, copying sentences

LESSON 6

Name _____

Part 1

Copy the sentences:

He will go with the man in that truck.

_____

Will Pat feed the cats?

_____

A steep hill had grass on it.

_____

Sand is still in the street.

_____

Part 2

(on) l i n r s t a n b c s o n a t h e h l u l o n e t a c k o n a e l i n o l s d o n r a o n a o n l e s t q

(for) o n f o r t s f o r l d t o t e f o r o r t a l f o r k f a n e f o r l p k d o f o r t a s f i l l w

(to) s o t o d p f o s a w t o k e t a o w a l t h t o s h t o u s h t r c t o j p i a t o e h l i t t o a

Part 3

Read the sentences in the box. Write the first word of these sentences.

1. The man told him, "Hop in this truck."	2nd sentence _____
2. "We do not have a clock," Jim said.	1st sentence _____
3. She said, "Fill this sack with fish."	3rd sentence _____

Writing sentences, finding words, writing words

6

Part 1

Match the words and complete them.

sing ———————●   ●——————— lo

hill ———————●   ●——————— ch

cheer ———————●   ●——————— sa

locks ———————●   ●——————— ng

sack ———————●   ●——————— ll

Part 2

Read the sentences in the box. Write the first word of these sentences.

1. Drop it in the box.
2. How much cash do you need?
3. That man has an old cat.

1st sentence _____

3rd sentence _____

2nd sentence _____

Part 3

Copy the sentences:

When they score, we will cheer.

_____

How well did she do in the math class?

_____

They sell chips and dip in that shop.

_____

Will you sell that horse?

_____

Writing words, copying sentences

Part 1

(**ch**)   o i s c h n d s n d r c h s h a d t h c h e s a i c h w h c r i t h r e i c h o p s h t c i c h e

(**th**)   u t o t h e o n i s n i d c h t h h e p t o s h t t o m e t h s h e t o h e s t h o l r s t h q w

(**ing**)   k m s d a i t o i n g r a t i s h i n g t m a t t o m e i n g s c i n p o i s x d i n g e r e s t

Part 2
Copy the sentences:

She is sending me to the meeting at the shop.

_____

We do not have the list with us.

_____

When the clocks stop, the bell will ring.

_____

The camp is at the top of that hill.

_____

Part 3
Match the words and complete them.

when	ch
chest	ift
crab	wh
fold	ab
lift	old

Finding letters, writing sentences, matching words

8

Part 1

Read the sentences in the box. Write the first word of these sentences.

1. When will we win a track meet?	2nd sentence _____
2. They were not singing.	3rd sentence _____
3. Can you get that truck to run?	1st sentence _____

Part 2

Copy the sentences:

The cow went faster than the old truck.

_____

That man was the last person on the bus.

_____

Bring them back to class in the morning.

_____

Run to the top of that hill.

_____

Part 3

Match the words and complete them.

chops	mu
crash	ops
much	el
clerk	cra
shell	erk

Writing words, writing sentences, matching words

Part 1

Copy the sentences:

Were you going to bring her letter with you?

_____

Jerry and I will have fish and chips for lunch.

_____

That woman went for a run this morning.

_____

After a nap, he felt much better.

_____

Part 2

Read the sentences in the box. Write the first word of these sentences.

1. Was she with him when you met her?
2. They sell clocks in that store.
3. Bring that glass of milk here.

1st sentence _____

3rd sentence _____

2nd sentence _____

Part 3

(was) h e w a s d i p s a w w a s i t w e s a w l e t t e r h o r s e w a s a t w a s w e s a w e n t

(you) w e y e s i f y o u w h a t t h e y t o f o r y o u o f w h a t y o w a s y o u i f o r a t o n

(er) a f t e r d r e s s c a t s o r e s e l l e r s h e l l s e t b a t t e r c l e r k g r e e t h e r

(this) a t t a p t h i s d a d t h i f t h i s p a n a m t h i s s h e t h e t h i s h

Writing sentences, writing words, finding words

Part 1

Match the words and complete them.

rancher ————————●   ●———————— th

going ————————●   ●———————— elf

path ————————●   ●———————— ranch

shelf ————————●   ●———————— go

Part 2

Copy the sentences:

The horse jumped over the creek.

_____

Tim fell into the creek when the horse jumped.

_____

Part 3

(**of**) o n f o r t h i s t o p o f a f t e r p o n d y o y h o r s e c o t o f t o l d o n o f y o u t o

(**said**) s a n d s i d s a i d h a d s a d s a i d s l i p s i t s a t s a i d s l o w s t o p s a i d s a w

(**how**) h o p h o t n o w h o w s h o p f l o w h o p h o w s h o t c o w h s l o w c r o w h o p

Part 4

Read the sentences in the box.   Write the last word of these sentences:

1. Just then, his sister yelled.
2. Where is the red broom?
3. He told her what to do.

2nd sentence _____

3rd sentence _____

1st sentence _____

Writing words, copying sentences, finding words, writing words

Part 1

Read the sentences in the box.   Write the last word of these sentences:

1. Tim went to the trash can.
2. His sister gave orders.
3. He began to sweep.

3rd sentence _____

1st sentence _____

2nd sentence _____

Part 2

Copy the sentences:

Tim got the broom and began to sweep.

_____

He told his sister what to do.

_____

His sister got mad and yelled at him.

_____

Part 3

(do) t h e t o i t d i m d o w a s d o d i d s e e d a d d o t o l d s i t d o c l i p i s d o t o

(one) c o r n o f t o d e e r o n e o r o n h i s o n e t o t o r n i t o n e s a d o n i t o n e

Part 4

Match the words and complete them.

where		tra
master		order
trash		mast
orders		ere

Writing words, copying sentences, finding words, matching words

Part 5

Tim Asked Questions

Tim asked a lot of questions. His dad told him to go to the	14
store for milk. Tim asked, "Which store?"	21
When his mom told him to set the cups on the shelf,	33
he asked, "Which shelf?"	37
His sister said, "Give me a hand."	44
Tim said, "Which hand?"	48
Last week, Tim was at a ranch. The rancher told him,	59
"Get on a horse and go down that path."	68
Tim asked 2 questions. What questions do you think he asked?	79
The rancher told Tim to get on a black horse, and Tim did that.	93
Then Tim went down the path and got to a creek.	104
He said, "How is this horse going to get over this creek?"	116

A Note to the Parent   Listen to the student read the passage. Count the number of words read in one minute and the number of errors.

Number of words read _____   Number of errors _____

We read the story _____ times.

(Parent's/Listener's) signature _____

Date _____

Reading fluency

Part 1

Copy the sentences:

She was wearing her slippers.

_____

He didn't wear socks on cold mornings.

_____

His mom told him what happened.

_____

Part 2

Read the sentences in the box.

Write the last word of these sentences:

1. These socks go with black slacks.
2. He had red socks for running.
3. His little sister grinned.
4. Ron's mom was not glad.

2nd sentence _____

4th sentence _____

3rd sentence _____

1st sentence _____

Part 3

Match the words and complete them.

there	per
asked	fore
before	ked
person	ere

Copying sentences, writing words, matching words

Part 4

Tim and His Big Sister

Tim's big sister did not ask questions. She gave orders.	10
She told her dog what to do. She told her pals what to do.	24
But when she told Tim what to do, he asked questions.	35
One day she said, "Get a broom and sweep the room."	46
Then Tim asked, "Which broom and which room?"	54
His sister said, "The red broom. Get that broom.	63
Then sweep this room."	67
Tim said, "Where is the red broom?"	74
His sister said, "It is next to the brown broom."	84
Do you know what Tim asked next?	91
Tim's sister said, "The brown broom is in the back room."	102
Tim got the broom and began to sweep.	110

A Note to the Parent

Listen to the student read the passage. Count the number of words read in one minute and the number of errors.

Number of words read _____   Number of errors _____

We read the story _____ times.

(Parent's/Listener's) signature _____

Date _____

Reading fluency

Part 1

Read the sentences in the box.

Write the last word of these sentences:

1. Get that ice out of my pocket.
2. At last, she stopped.
3. Now I will help you.
4. How did she do that?

4th sentence _____

2nd sentence _____

1st sentence _____

3rd sentence _____

Part 2

Match the words and complete them.

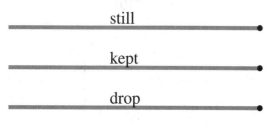

still   pt

kept   ill

drop   ll

well   dr

Part 3

Copy the sentences:

He had a big chunk of ice in his bag.

_____

She helped the rat hop.

_____

How do you think she did that?

_____

Writing words, matching words, copying sentences

Part 4

Ron's Socks

On a cold morning, Ron went to his mom and said,	11
"I have no socks."	15
His mom said, "You have lots and lots of socks. You have	27
red socks for running and socks that go with black slacks."	38
"No, Mom," Ron said. "I do not have one sock in my room."	51
Ron's mom said, "If sock robbing is going on, I'll get a cop."	64
She did just that. The cop went in Ron's room and said,	76
"There are no socks in this room. There must be sock robbers	88
in this town." Then the cop said, "I will get more cops." Soon,	101
there were 18 cops in Ron's room.	108
One cop said, "We need dogs to track down the sock robbers."	120

A Note to the Parent   Listen to the student read the passage. Count the number of words read in one minute and the number of errors.

Number of words read _____   Number of errors _____

We read the story _____ times.

(Parent's/Listener's) signature _____

Date _____

Reading fluency

Part 1

(ed)   a f t e r e d t u s h e d r l h e r l o e d p n m c v e d w r e r a e s t o u e d b c f e r i e d

(lie)   c h l i d s l i e d i d n o g u m l i e n o t h e l i e s a t l i p l i e l i f t l i e s l o w

(are)   h o w t h e n a n t a r e a n d a r e r e d c a b a t r a m s a r e r a t s a n t a r e a n

Part 2

The words in the first column have endings.
Write the same words without endings in the second column.

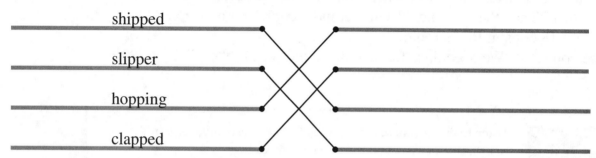

shipped

slipper

hopping

clapped

Part 3

Read the sentences in the box.   Write the last word of these sentences:

1. Sandy went to the store.
2. The rat ate at a fast rate.
3. She gave the rat oats.
4. The rat chomped and chomped.

4th sentence _____

1st sentence _____

3rd sentence _____

2nd sentence _____

Part 4

Copy this sentence:

She gave the rat oats with gum on them.

_____

Finding words, inflectional suffixes, writing words, copying sentences

Part 5

Kit, the Kangaroo

Kit was a kangaroo. Kangaroos hop. Kit hopped as well	10
as the best kangaroos. But one day, she stopped hopping.	20
She said, "I can not hop." She was very sad.	30
A little rat was sitting next to Kit. He said, "I can help	43
you hop."	45
Kit asked, "How can you do that?"	52
The rat said, "Let me show you how. I will be back soon.	65
And when I get back, you will hop as well as you	77
ever hopped before."	80
When the rat got back, he had a big bag. He said,	92
"This will fix you up."	97
He had a big chunk of ice in the bag. He dropped	109
the ice in Kit's pocket. As soon as he dropped the ice,	121
Kit began to hop.	125

A Note to the Parent   Listen to the student read the passage. Count the number of words read in one minute and the number of errors.

Number of words read _____   Number of errors _____

We read the story _____ times.

(Parent's/Listener's) signature _____

Date _____

Reading fluency

Part 1

Read the sentences in the box.   Write the last word of these sentences:

1. She got a rat that ate.
2. That rat ate at a fast rate.
3. Sandy dropped the rat into a box.
4. The rat bit Sandy on the nose.

4th sentence _____

1st sentence _____

3rd sentence _____

2nd sentence _____

Part 2

ea s e e m t o e a h e a r h e a l r a t e h e r e a r s e r a e s t o w e a t c f e a i e d

too c h o f a t o o i e d i d t o o f o r l i e n o t t o o e s a t o o o n l i e t o t o o i e s l o w

who h o w t h e n a t a r e w h o m n a r e w h o z c a b e w h o i t y u w h o n g h o w a r i a

Part 3

The words in the first column have endings.
Write the same words without endings in the second column.

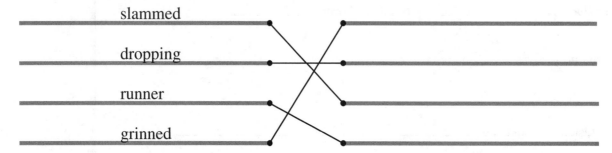

slammed

dropping

runner

grinned

Part 4

Copy this sentence:

The fat rat ate oats for seven days.

_____

Part 5

The Rat That Had a Fast Rate

Sandy had a rat that ate fast. She said, "That rat eats	12
too much, I must make the rat slow down."	21
Sandy went to the store and got ten packs of gum. She said,	34
"I will smear the gum on the oats." Then she gave the oats	47
to the rat. "Here are some oats," she said. "You will have	59
fun eating them."	62
The rat began eating at a very fast rate. But then the rate	75
began to go down.	79
The rat chomped and chomped. The rat said, "I like oats,	90
but these oats are not fun. I am chomping as fast as I can,	104
but the oats don't go down."	110
Sandy said, "Ho, ho. There is gum on them so that you	122
cannot eat at a fast rate."	128

A Note to the Parent

Listen to the student read the passage. Count the number of words read in one minute and the number of errors.

Number of words read _____   Number of errors _____

We read the story _____ times.

(Parent's/Listener's) signature _____

Date _____

Reading fluency

LESSON 17

Name _____

Part 1

Copy the sentences:

The camp woman gave him a hammer.

_____

She fixed the lamp.

_____

The tramp did not answer.

_____

Part 2

The words in the first column have endings.
Write the same words without endings in the second column.

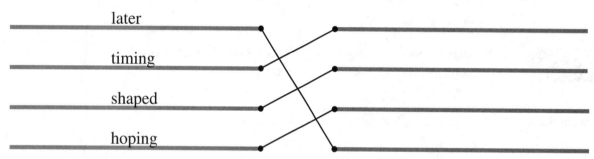

later

timing

shaped

hoping

Part 3

(oa) a s w h e b t o e a h e a o a h e a t o a d o o a e a o l o a r e e s t o a e r u w f o a i h o o

(for) f i l l f o r f e e d s f o r t o r n f o r t o o f s a t f o r l i e a t o f o f i s h o r

(make) h o w t h e m a k e m a d w h o m a k e h o w m a k e m a d e i t m a k e m a n s l e m

Copying sentences, inflectional suffixes, finding words

22

Name _____

Part 4

Sandy's Plan for the Rat's Fast Rate

Sandy's rat ate at a fast rate. The rat ran at a fast rate.	14
And it even hopped at a fast rate. Sandy had a plan to make	28
the rat's rate go down.	33
Sandy got a rat that did not eat at a fast rate and did not run fast.	50
This rat was fat. It sat and sat. When this rat ate, it chomped slowly.	65
Sandy said, "I will take this slow rat and show my fast rat	78
how to be slow." Sandy dropped the fat rat into the box	90
with the fast rat.	94
The fast rat said, "This fat rat needs help. It is too fat.	107
I will show it how to go fast."	115
Sandy's rat bit the fat rat on the nose. "Stop that," he said.	128

A Note to the Parent

Listen to the student read the passage. Count the number of words read in one minute and the number of errors.

Number of words read _____   Number of errors _____

We read the story _____ times.

(Parent's/Listener's) signature _____

Date _____

Reading fluency

Part 1

The words in the first column have endings.
Write the same words without endings in the second column.

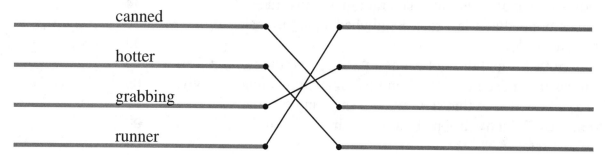

canned _____

hotter _____

grabbing _____

runner _____

Part 2

Copy the sentences:

The man with the faster rate will win.

_____

I can even take a bath faster than you.

_____

Part 3

Match the words and complete them.

their _____   _____ ld

women _____   _____ th

held _____   _____ sh

show _____   _____ men

Part 4

(day) a s d a d d a y b a d d a y a t b i d d i d o n d e e r d a y a f t e r d a y d e n t d o

(bath) b a c k b a t h b a g b i t p a t h b a t h f o r b e a t s a t f o r b e d b a t h b r o o m

(soon) h o w t h e s o o n t o o s o o n r o o m o f m a k e s o o n b r o o m s o o n s a n d o n

Inflectional suffixes, copying sentences, writing words, finding words

Part 5

The Tramp at the Camp

A tramp went down a road. He came to a camp.	11
He stopped and said, "I hate to work, but I need to eat.	24
So I will see if I can get a job at this camp." So the	39
tramp went to the woman who ran the camp.	48
The tramp said, "Can I work at this camp?	57
I can do lots of jobs."	63
The camp woman said, "You are a tramp."	71
The tramp said, "Yes, but I am a champ at camp work."	83
"Can you fix lamps?"	87
"Yes," the tramp said.	91
"Can you make boat ramps?"	96
"Yes," said the tramp. "I am the champ at ramps."	106
The camp woman said, "Then I will let you work in this	118
camp." The camp woman gave the tramp a hammer. She said,	129
"Take this hammer and make a ramp for the boats."	139

A Note to the Parent

Listen to the student read the passage. Count the number of words read in one minute and the number of errors.

Number of words read _____   Number of errors _____

We read the story _____ times.

(Parent's/Listener's) signature _____

Date _____

Reading fluency

Part 1

The words in the first column have endings.
Write the same words without endings in the second column.

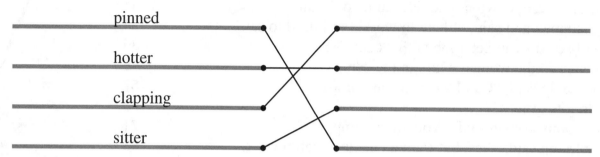

pinned

hotter

clapping

sitter

Part 2

Read the sentences in the box.

1. The tramp said, "I am your brother."
2. He said, "You need boaters."
3. The camp woman clapped.

Write the last word of these sentences:

2nd sentence _____

1st sentence _____

3rd sentence _____

Part 3

Match the words and complete them.

smell   eer

stand   ell

cheer   th

bath   st

Part 4

Copy the sentences:

The camp woman held her nose.

_____

Bob bent down and began to paddle.

_____

Part 5

The Tramp Has a Meeting with Sam

The tramp slept at the table. The next day he woke up	12
and felt rested. He went to the woman who ran the camp.	24
The woman held her nose as she said, "You smell, tramp.	35
Will you take a bath?"	40
"No," the tramp said.	44
Just then, a big man named Sam came up. He held	55
his nose and said, "Tramp, you are not the champ worker	66
at this camp. I am."	71
A woman said, "Let's have a meet between the tramp and Sam."	83
So the men and women set things up for the big meet.	95
They gave a tamping pole to each man. They said, "We will	107
see how well this tramp can tamp."	114
They went to the hill. The camp woman said, "Take these	125
tamping poles and see how fast you can pound the ruts from	137
this path."	139

A Note to the Parent — Listen to the student read the passage. Count the number of words read in one minute and the number of errors.

Number of words read _____   Number of errors _____

We read the story _____ times.

(Parent's/Listener's) signature _____

Date _____

Reading fluency

LESSON 20

Name _____

Part 1

Read the question and fill in the circle next to the best answer.
Write the answer in the blank.

1. The tramp said, "I can not open this door. This door has a _____ on it."

   ○ handle   ○ note   ○ lock   ○ top

2. Big Bob said, "I will _____ the door in."

   ○ fix   ○ kick   ○ pick   ○ lock

3. The old man held a _____ to his ear.

   ○ pick   ○ handle   ○ horn   ○ top

4. Big Bob said, "Make a _____ for the old man."

   ○ clock   ○ lock   ○ horn   ○ note

Part 2

The words in the first column have endings.
Write the same words without endings in the second column.

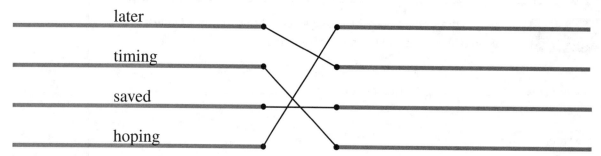

later

timing

saved

hoping

Part 3

Copy the sentence:

The tramp grabbed the handle of the door.

_____

The old man hit the lock with a hammer.

_____

Answering questions, inflectional suffixes, copying sentences
Directions, Part 1: Read the directions to the student. "Read the question and fill in the circle next to the answer. Write the answer in the blank."

28

Name _____

Part 4

The Tramp's Brother Has a Boat Meet

One day another tramp came to the camp. This tramp	10
was big and fat. He smelled as bad as a goat.	21
He went up to the camp woman and said, "My name is Bob.	34
I do not like to work, but I have to eat. And I am	48
the best worker you have seen."	54
The tramp that was champ of the camp went up to	65
the camp woman and said, "That is Big Bob, my brother."	76
Big Bob said, "No. You can't be my brother. My brother	87
is fat, and he smells. But you are not fat, and you do not smell."	102
The tramp said, "But I am your brother."	110
The camp woman said, "We do not need more workers in this camp."	123
The tramp said, "But you need boaters. And Big Bob is the best	136
there is."	138

A Note to the Parent

Listen to the student read the passage. Count the number of words read in one minute and the number of errors.

Number of words read _____   Number of errors _____

We read the story _____ times.

(Parent's/Listener's) signature _____

Date _____

Reading fluency

Part 1

Read the question and fill in the circle next to the answer.
Write the answer in the blank.

1. The con man had a box of _____.

   ○ locks   ○ clocks   ○ mops   ○ tops

2. The tramp was a fast _____ raker.

   ○ slope   ○ slop   ○ shore   ○ shop

3. The tramp said, "I will _____ this mop near the door."

   ○ prop   ○ slop   ○ stop   ○ bop

4. The con man sold the camp woman _____ mops.

   ○ seven   ○ thin   ○ 50   ○ bad

Part 2

The words in the first column have endings.
Write the same words without endings in the second column.

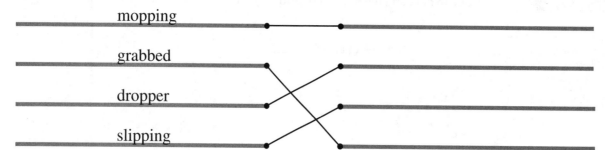

_____   mopping   ●————————————●   _____

_____   grabbed   ●   ●   _____

_____   dropper   ●   ●   _____

_____   slipping   ●   ●   _____

Part 3

Copy the sentence:

The con man was glad to sell the mops.

_____

Answering questions, inflectional suffixes, copying sentences

Part 4

The Clock Maker at the Camp

The tramp and his brother Big Bob went to the shed. The	12
tramp grabbed the handle of the door. He said, "This door has a	25
lock on it. How will we get in the shed? The hammers and the	39
tamping poles are in the shed. We need hammers and tampers	50
if we are to work."	55
Big Bob said, "Brother, don't bother with that lock. I will	66
kick the door in."	70
"No," the tramp said. "Let's go to the camp woman and see	82
if she can get in this shed."	89
So they went to the camp woman. The camp woman said, "I will	102
get a man to fix that lock."	109
Later, an old man came to the camp. He had a big bag and a	124
big horn that he held to his ear.	132
He said, "I am here to fix the clock."	141

A Note to the Parent   Listen to the student read the passage. Count the number of words read in one minute and the number of errors.

Number of words read _____   Number of errors _____

We read the story _____ times.

(Parent's/Listener's) signature _____

Date _____

Reading fluency

Part 1

Match the words and complete them.

matter   cause

because   ck

lifted   ed

shack   mat

Part 2

Copy the sentences:

Cathy worked in a dress shop.

_____

Cathy and Pam left the shed and sat on a bench.

_____

Part 3

Read the question and fill in the circle next to the answer.
Write the answer in the blank.

1. Pam led Cathy to a _____.

   ◯ dress shop   ◯ big camp   ◯ clock store   ◯ fish shed

2. The man in a big coat said, "I am a _____."

   ◯ cook   ◯ worker   ◯ fish packer   ◯ slop raker

3. The man had a basket of fish in his _____.

   ◯ shed   ◯ boat   ◯ shop   ◯ store

4. The man in the fish shed gave Pam and Cathy _____ chips.

   ◯ free   ◯ five   ◯ fish   ◯ flat

Writing words, copying sentences, answering questions

Name _____

Part 4

The Tramp Meets the Con Man

A con man came to the camp. That con man came up the camp	14
road with a box. The camp woman met him.	23
The con man dropped his box and held the lid up. He grabbed a	37
mop from the box. He said, "The workers will like this mop. It	50
is fatter than other mops. So a worker can mop faster	61
with this mop."	64
The camp woman said, "I will get someone to take that mop and	77
see how well it works." So the camp woman yelled for the tramp.	90
The tramp was on a slope near a shore of the lake. Was he	104
making a ramp? No, he was raking slop near the pond. He was a	118
fast slop raker. He went to the con man and the camp woman.	131

A Note to the Parent

Listen to the student read the passage. Count the number of words read in one minute and the number of errors.

Number of words read _____   Number of errors _____

We read the story _____ times.

(Parent's/Listener's) signature _____

Date _____

Reading fluency

Part 1

The words in the first column have endings.
Write the same words without endings in the second column.

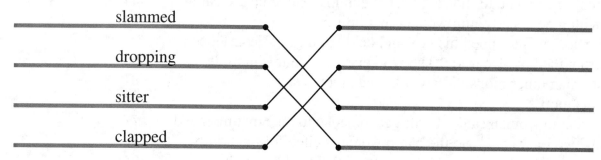

slammed

dropping

sitter

clapped

Part 2

Read the question and fill in the circle next to the answer.
Write the answer in the blank.

1. When Gretta said, "Ho, ho," Chee _____.

   ○ made a note   ○ sat near the door   ○ became very mad

2. Chee asked Gretta, "Did you _____ at your job?"

   ○ work fast   ○ feel sad   ○ have fun   ○ sell fish

Part 3

Copy these sentences:

She got better and better at saying things.

_____

I don't like to stay at home.

_____

He will get a job, too.

_____

Inflectional suffixes, answering questions, copying sentences

Part 4

Cathy and a Band at the Bend

Cathy worked in a dress shop. One day she said, "I need a	13
rest." So she went to her pal, Pam. She said, "Pam, let us go	27
to hear a band play. A band is near the bend in the road. They	42
play well."	45
Then Cathy and Pam went to hear the band. When they got near	58
the bend in the road, Pam said, "I need to eat. Let me lead you	73
to a little shed. It is near the stream. They sell fish and chips	87
in that shed."	90
So Pam led Cathy to the fish shed near the stream. The	102
shack was packed with folks. The folks were yelling, "I was	113
next. Give me my order of fish and chips."	122
Pam said, "This is a mess."	128
Cathy and Pam left the fish shed and sat on a bench.	140

A Note to the Parent

Listen to the student read the passage. Count the number of words read in one minute and the number of errors.

Number of words read _____   Number of errors _____

We read the story _____ times.

(Parent's/Listener's) signature _____

Date _____

Reading fluency

Part 1

The words in the first column have endings.
Write the same words without endings in the second column.

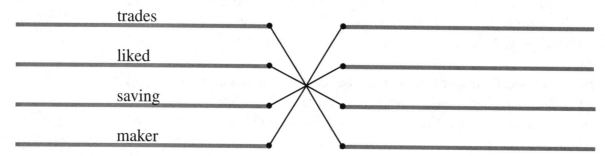

trades

liked

saving

maker

Part 2

Read the question and fill in the circle next to the answer.
Write the answer in the blank.

1. The clock maker did not _____ well.

  ◯ see   ◯ read   ◯ hear   ◯ feel

2. The con man said, "We will _____ in the shade."

  ◯ stay   ◯ sit   ◯ play   ◯ work

3. The clock maker said, "I will not _____ this horn."

  ◯ sell   ◯ play   ◯ pack   ◯ trade

4. The clock maker handed his _____ to the con man.

  ◯ little horn   ◯ corn   ◯ big horn   ◯ pack

Part 3

Copy these sentences:

The con man dressed up like a corn grower.

_____

He stamped up and down.

_____

Inflectional suffixes, answering questions, copying sentences

Part 4

Chee, the Dog

Gretta got a little dog. She named the dog Chee. Chee got	12
bigger and bigger each day.	17
On a very cold day, Gretta said, "Chee, I must go to the	30
store. You stay home. I will be back."	38
Chee said, "Store, lots, of, for, no."	45
Then Gretta said, "Did I hear that dog say things?"	55
Chee said, "Say things can I do."	62
Gretta said, "Dogs don't say things. So I must not hear	73
things well."	75
But Chee did say things. Gretta left the dog at home. When	87
Gretta came back, Chee was sitting near the door.	96
Gretta said, "That dog is bigger than she was."	105
Then the dog said, "Read, read for me of left."	115
Gretta said, "Is that dog saying that she can read?"	125
Gretta got a pad and made a note for the dog.	136
The note said, "Dear Chee, if you can read this note,	147
I will hand you a bag of bones."	155

A Note to the Parent

Listen to the student read the passage. Count the number of words read in one minute and the number of errors.

Number of words read _____   Number of errors _____

We read the story _____ times.

(Parent's/Listener's) signature _____

Date _____

Reading fluency

LESSON 25

Part 1

Match the words and complete them.

_____ felt _____   _____ ft _____

_____ help _____   _____ lf _____

_____ left _____   _____ lt _____

_____ self _____   _____ he _____

Part 2

Copy the sentences:

Chee began to say odd things.

_____

She left her home to get a job.

_____

He had tears on his cheeks.

_____

The man came back with his boss.

_____

Part 3

The words in the first column have endings.
Write the same words without endings in the second column.

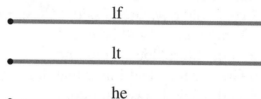

_____ getting _____   _____

_____ dropper _____   _____

_____ grabbed _____   _____

_____ bigger _____   _____

Writing words, copying sentences, inflectional suffixes

Part 4

The Old Clock Maker and the Con Man

The old clock maker did not hear well. He left the camp	12
with the lock. He had the lock in his pack. He went down the road	27
from the camp. Then he met a corn grower.	36
But the corn grower was not a corn grower. He was the con man	50
dressed up like a corn grower. The con man liked conning folks.	62
The con man said, "Let's go sit in the shade near my shed."	75
"Yes," the clock maker said, "I will trade for a bed."	86
"No, not a bed," the con man said. "Shed. We will sit near the shed."	101
The clock maker said, "Yes, I like a sled, but I don't see a sled."	116
The con man was mad at the clock maker. He yelled, "WE WILL	129
SIT IN THE SHADE."	133
"Yes," the clock maker said. "I am ready to trade."	143

A Note to the Parent

Listen to the student read the passage. Count the number of words read in one minute and the number of errors.

Number of words read _____   Number of errors _____

We read the story _____ times.

(Parent's/Listener's) signature _____

Date _____

Reading fluency

Part 1

Read the words in the box. Then fill in the blanks.

worked	well	rode	named	fast
good	best	swam	ran	bent

There was a ranch in the West. The rancher who _____ this ranch was _____

Emma Branch. She rode a horse _____ . She chopped _____ and she swam faster.

The men and women who _____ for Emma Branch liked her. They said, "She is the

_____ in the West."

Part 2

The words in the first column have endings.
Write the same words without endings in the second column.

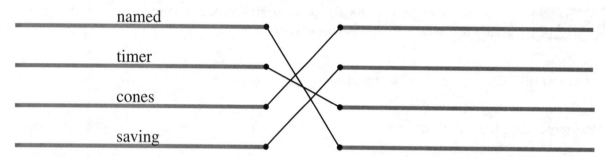

named

timer

cones

saving

Part 3

Copy the sentences:

She checked up on the workers.

_____

Get ready to leave now.

_____

This horse is very tame.

_____

Vocabulary/context clues, inflectional suffixes, copying sentences

Part 4

Chee Goes for a Job

Chee felt sad. So she left her home to get a job.	12
Chee went to a fire station. She went up to the man who ran	26
the station and said, "I need a job. Can you help me?"	38
The man said, "Is my hearing going bad or did that dog say	51
something to me?"	54
The dog said, "I did say something. Do you have a	65
job for me?"	68
The man said, "Ho, ho. That dog is saying things, but dogs	80
can't speak."	82
Chee got so mad that she began to say odd things. "Fire	94
station for of to go," she said.	101
The man said, "Ho, ho. This dog is fun. I will keep this dog	115
with me. I like to hear the odd things that dog can say."	128
Chee was so mad at the fireman she said, "From of for, fireman."	141

A Note to the Parent

Listen to the student read the passage. Count the number of words read in one minute and the number of errors.

Number of words read _____ Number of errors _____

We read the story _____ times.

(Parent's/Listener's) signature _____

Date _____

Reading fluency

Part 1

Read the words in the box. Then fill in the blanks.

fastest	packer	stick	plant	old
stackers	slowest	odd	mad	slate
pack	made	slat	job	stack

Chee got a _____ at a _____ plant. When she was not _____, she did

not say _____ things. The woman who ran the _____ showed Chee how to

_____ slate. At the end of one year, Chee was one of the fastest _____.

Part 2

Copy the sentences:

The woman showed Chee how to stack slate.

_____

She worked at the plant for nearly a year.

_____

Set that slab on top of the pile.

_____

Part 3

The words in the first column have endings.
Write the same words without endings in the second column.

_____ clapped

_____ running

_____ swimmer

_____ biggest

Vocabulary/context clues, copying sentences, inflectional suffixes

Part 4

The Rancher

There was a big ranch in the West. The rancher who ran this	13
ranch was named Emma Branch. She rode a horse well.	23
She chopped fast, and she swam faster. The men and women	34
who worked for Emma Branch liked her. They said, "She is the	46
best in the West." On her ranch she had sheep and she had cows.	60
There were goats and horses. There was a lot of grass.	71
The rancher had a lot of women and men working for her. They	84
worked with the sheep and the goats, and they milked the cows.	96
Each worker had a horse. But the rancher's horse was the biggest	108
and the best. It was a big, black horse named Flop.	119
Flop got its name because it reared up. When Flop reared up,	131
any rider on it fell down and went "flop" in the grass.	143

A Note to the Parent   Listen to the student read the passage. Count the number of words read in one minute and the number of errors.

Number of words read _____   Number of errors _____

We read the story _____ times.

(Parent's/Listener's) signature _____

Date _____

Reading fluency

Part 1

Read the words in the box. Then fill in the blanks.

leave	shop	sheep	sacks	best
steal	work	shave	plan	faster
packs	shears	wool	well	fake

The con man said, "I can _____ a sheep before it sees the _____. You can

_____, but you cannot get someone who can shave _____ than me."

The con man told the rancher to get him ten _____ for holding the _____. He

did not plan to shear _____. He planned to _____ them.

Part 2

Match the words and complete them.

before	est
steal	st
still	eal
chest	fore

Part 3

Copy the sentences:

He got the shears from his pack.

_____

He planned to pack sheep into sacks.

_____

The rancher sat on the con man and shaved his locks.

_____

Vocabulary/context clues, writing words, copying sentences

Part 4

Chee Stacks Slate

Chee went to get a job, but no plant had jobs for dogs that	14
say things. At last, Chee went to a slate plant. Chee said,	26
"I hope that I can get a job here." Chee went into the plant.	40
Chee went past stacks of slate. She came to the woman	51
who ran the plant. Chee asked, "Do you have a job I can do	65
in this plant?"	68
The woman looked at Chee. Then the woman said, "Ho, ho, ho.	80
I cannot help going 'Ho, ho, ho.'"	87
Chee got so mad that she began to say odd things. "Stop slate	100
for from me, of go so no to do, ho ho."	111
The woman fell down and kept going, "Ho, ho, ho."	121
Chee felt so mad that she did not stop saying odd things.	133
The woman got sore from going "ho, ho, ho."	142
She had lots of tears on her cheeks.	150

A Note to the Parent   Listen to the student read the passage. Count the number of words read in one minute and the number of errors.

Number of words read _____   Number of errors _____

We read the story _____ times.

(Parent's/Listener's) signature _____

Date _____

Reading fluency

Part 1

Read the words in the box. Then fill in the blanks.

tamps	ranch	rest	pack	old
odd	slop	camp	say	stay
sack	ramps	hill	lake	leave

The tramp worked at the _____ for nearly a year. He tamped and made _____.

Now he said, "I will _____ this camp. Tramps don't _____ in a camp for more

than a year."

So the tramp got his _____. He told the camp woman, "The work here is getting

_____, and I need a _____."

Part 2

The words in the first column have endings.
Write the same words without endings in the second column.

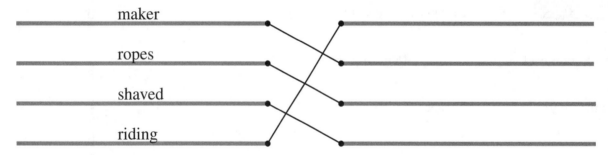

maker

ropes

shaved

riding

Part 3

Copy the sentences:

He worked there for nearly a year.

_____

When the sun comes up, he will shear sheep.

_____

Vocabulary/context clues, inflectional suffixes, copying sentences

Part 4

The Con Man and the Sheep Rancher

Emma Branch had a lot of big sheep on her ranch. One day	13
she said, "My sheep need shearing. I will send for a sheep shearer."	26
So she told one of her helpers to go to town and get someone	40
who can shear sheep. The helper went down the road to town. But	53
he did not get there. He met the con man on the road. The con man	69
said, "Where are you going?"	74
The helper said, "The rancher needs her sheep sheared."	83
The con man said, "I am the best at shearing sheep. I have	96
shears in my pack."	100
So Emma's helper led the con man back to the ranch. When they	113
got there, Emma yelled from the door, "I hope that man can shear fast."	127
The con man said, "I can shear sheep. I can shape. And I can shear."	142
"But how is your rate at shearing?" the rancher asked.	152
"I can go so fast that I can shave a sheep before it sees the shears."	168

A Note to the Parent

Listen to the student read the passage. Count the number of words read in one minute and the number of errors.

Number of words read _____   Number of errors _____

We read the story _____ times.

(Parent's/Listener's) signature _____

Date _____

Reading fluency

Part 1

Read the question and fill in the circle next to the answer.
Write the answer in the blank.

1. The tramp was sleeping near a sheep _____.

　○ camp　　○ shed　　○ shop　　○ ranch

2. The tramp felt more like _____ than shearing.

　○ sweeping　　○ shaving　　○ yelling　　○ sleeping

3. Emma said, "You have _____ minutes to shear _____ sheep."

　○ five　　○ 50　　○ 20　　○ ten

4. Emma kept her _____ with the tramp.

　○ plan　　○ ranch　　○ deal　　○ hand

Part 2

Copy the sentences:

The sun came up in the morning.

_____

The cook will make a good meal.

_____

Part 3

The words in the first column have endings.
Write the same words without endings in the second column.

sweeping

reached

helper

Answering questions, copying sentences, inflectional suffixes

Part 4

The Rancher and the Tramp

The tramp had worked at the camp for nearly a year. He had	13
tamped and made ramps. He had fixed lamps and raked slop	24
near the lake. But now he said, "I think I will leave this camp.	38
I am a tramp, and tramps don't stay in a camp for more than a year."	54
So the tramp got his pack and went to the camp woman. He told her,	69
"I must go now. The work here is getting old, and I need a rest."	84
So the tramp left and went down the camp road. When he got	97
to a town, he said, "I see a person on a big, black horse. I will ask	114
that rider where I can go to rest in the shade."	125

A Note to the Parent   Listen to the student read the passage. Count the number of words read in one minute and the number of errors.

Number of words read _____   Number of errors _____

We read the story _____ times.

(Parent's/Listener's) signature _____

Date _____

Reading fluency

Part 1

Match the words and complete them.

slow •————————————•	year
shame •————————————•	to
town •————————————•	sha
yearly •————————————•	ow

Part 2

Copy the sentences:

He got slower and slower with each meal that he ate.

_____

Emma went to town and bragged.

_____

Part 3

Read the words in the box. Then fill in the blanks.

like	rested	said	mean	time
best	look	shave	shape	shade
bad	meet	good	neat	seem

The rancher said, "We will have the _____ at the end of this week. So get in

_____."

"Yes, yes," the fat tramp said.

"I _____ it," the rancher said. "You _____ to be in _____ shape. You

have _____ for seven weeks. Now you don't _____ like you can do things very

fast."

Part 4

The Tramp Shows the Rancher How to Shear

The sun came up in the morning. The tramp was sleeping	11
near a big sheep shed. The rancher's helper came to wake him up.	24
The tramp said, "Leave me be. I am sleeping." So the	35
tramp went back to sleep.	40
The helper ran to Emma and said, "That tramp didn't get up	52
when I went to wake him up."	59
Emma grabbed shears and ran over to the tramp. The helper	70
ran with her. When they got to the tramp, the rancher	81
handed the shears to her helper. She said to the tramp, "If you	94
don't get up, my helper will give you a shearing."	104
So the tramp got up and went to the sheep shed with Emma.	117
Emma said, "We have a deal. If you can shear 50 sheep as fast	131
as you hammer, you may stay and rest on my ranch."	142
Then she handed the shears to the tramp.	150

A Note to the Parent

Listen to the student read the passage. Count the number of words read in one minute and the number of errors.

Number of words read _____   Number of errors _____

We read the story _____ times.

(Parent's/Listener's) signature _____

Date _____

Reading fluency

Part 1

Read the question and fill in the circle next to the answer.
Write the answer in the blank.

1. Shelly made a _____ of wool as big as a hill.

   ○ pack   ○ sheer   ○ heap   ○ sweep

2. The tramp made a pile of wool as big as a _____ sheep.

   ○ little   ○ fatter   ○ big   ○ short

3. Emma said to the tramp, "You will _____ like a horse."

   ○ run   ○ go   ○ rest   ○ work

4. The tramp had never been _____ in a meet before.

   ○ shaved   ○ beaten   ○ broken   ○ picked

Part 2

The words in the first column have endings.
Write the same words without endings in the second column.

melted _____

working _____

beaten _____

slower _____

Part 3

Copy the sentences:

She showed the others how fast she was.

_____

He ate big meals of ham and beans.

_____

Answering questions, inflectional suffixes, copying sentences

Part 4

The Rancher Sets Up a Shearing Meet

The tramp had stayed at the ranch for seven weeks. Every	11
day, he had big meals of beef and ham and beans and corn. Every	25
day, he sat in the shade near the lake. And every day, he got a	40
little fatter. He got slower and slower with each meal that he ate.	53
The rancher did not think that the tramp was slow. She had	65
seen him go so fast that the helper did not sweep the wool as	79
fast as the tramp shaved sheep.	85
Emma went to town and bragged. She said, "There is a tramp on	98
my ranch that can shear sheep faster than anyone you have seen."	110
When Emma was in town one day, she told a lot of people,	123
"My tramp can beat anyone in a shearing meet."	132
A woman named Shelly stepped up to Emma and said, "I think	144
I can beat anyone in a shearing meet."	152

A Note to the Parent

Listen to the student read the passage. Count the number of words read in one minute and the number of errors.

Number of words read _____   Number of errors _____

We read the story _____ times.

(Parent's/Listener's) signature _____

Date _____

Reading fluency

Part 1

The words in the first column have endings.
Write the same words without endings in the second column.

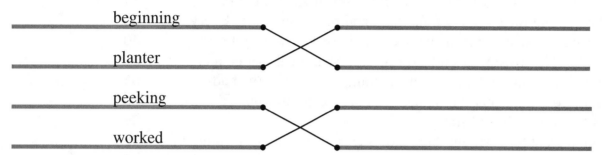

beginning

planter

peeking

worked

Part 2

Read the words in the box. Then fill in the blanks.

shaping	shaving	faster	week	work
fatter	sore	sheared	hot	meals
cold	hands	hammer	made	shape

The rancher gave the tramp more work. At the end of the day, the tramp was _____.

But at the end of the week, he began to get _____. His _____ began to go like

a flash. His shears began to get _____ when he was _____ sheep. The tramp was

beginning to get back in _____.

Part 3

Copy the sentences:

His hammer began to go like a flash.

_____

There was no more work at the ranch.

_____

Inflectional suffixes, vocabulary/context clues, copying sentences

Part 4

The Shearing Meet

The rancher had told the tramp to get in shape for the shearing	13
meet. But did the tramp get in shape? No. He ate big meals	26
of corn and ham and beans and meat.	34
Was the tramp in shape at the end of the week? No. The tramp	48
was out of shape and very slow.	55
The people from town came to the ranch with Shelly.	65
Shelly was in tip-top shape. Before the meet began, she	75
sheared a sheep to show the others how fast she was.	86
Before the wool that fell from the sheep landed, the sheep	97
was shaved from one end to the other.	105
The people cheered. "Shelly can beat anyone at shearing,"	114
they yelled.	116
The tramp had to work to pick up the shears. He said,	128
"I may have rested too much, but when I get going,	139
I will speed up."	143
The rancher said, "Shelly and the tramp will shear all day."	154

A Note to the Parent

Listen to the student read the passage. Count the number of words read in one minute and the number of errors.

Number of words read _____   Number of errors _____

We read the story _____ times.

(Parent's/Listener's) signature _____

Date _____

Reading fluency

Part 1

Read the question and fill in the circle next to the answer.
Write the answer in the blank.

1. Shelly said, "I have never been _____ in a shearing meet."

○ broken   ○ cheered   ○ beaten   ○ shaved

2. At the end of the meet, the tramp had sheared _____ sheep.

○ 5000   ○ 9000   ○ 210   ○ 501

3. Shelly had sheared _____ sheep.

○ 5000   ○ 9000   ○ 210   ○ 501

Part 2

The words in the first column have endings.
Write the same words without endings in the second column.

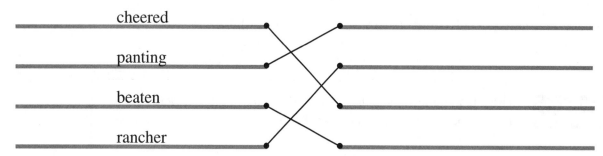

cheered

panting

beaten

rancher

Part 3

Copy the sentences:

She is the best worker at the plant.

_____

The people from town waved to the tramp.

_____

Her helpers began to bag the wool.

_____

Answering questions, inflectional suffixes, copying sentences

Part 4

The Tramp Gets in Shape

The tramp worked and worked at the ranch. Every day, he got	12
up when the sun was peeking over the hill in the east. The tramp	26
did not eat a big meal. He went to the sheep shed and sheared	40
sheep. Then he picked corn. Then he ate a little meal. He had an	54
egg and a little bit of ham. He said, "I need more to eat."	68
"No more," the rancher said. "Back to work for you." She	79
handed the tramp a hammer. "Take boards and make a gate,"	90
she said.	92
After the tramp had made a gate, the rancher said, "Now	103
take boards and make a pen for goats." After the tramp had made	116
a pen of boards, she said, "Next, you're going to dig holes for	129
planting trees."	131
So the tramp dug tree holes. Then he planted trees. Then he	143
sheared more sheep. At last, the rancher said, "Now you may	154
eat a meal."	157

> **A Note to the Parent**
>
> Listen to the student read the passage. Count the number of words read in one minute and the number of errors.
>
> Number of words read _____   Number of errors _____
>
> We read the story _____ times.
>
> (Parent's/Listener's) signature _____
>
> Date _____

Reading fluency

Part 1

Read the words in the box. Then fill in the blanks.

day	packer	speed	rate	packing	plant
quit	week	stacking	year	shearing	rat
stacker	shack	leave	slacks	sick	time

Chee worked as a slate _____ for nearly a year. By then, her _____ of

_____ was very good. But she was getting a little _____ of her job. "Stack, stack,

stack," she said. "It's time to do something else." So she went to the woman who ran the slate

_____ and said, "I think I have to _____ and get another job."

Part 2

The words in the first column have endings.
Write the same words without endings in the second column.

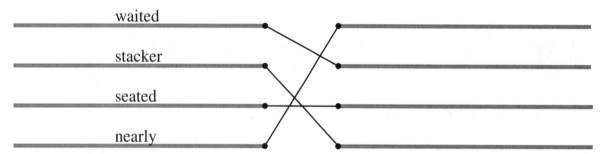

waited

stacker

seated

nearly

Part 3

Match the words and complete them.

something   some

person   low

yellow   ts

coats   per

Part 4

The Meet with Shelly Is Set

The tramp felt he was in shape for the shearing meet. When	12
there was no more work on Emma's ranch, the tramp did some	24
work at the next ranch, so he could stay in shape. He made ten	38
gates. He planted 600 trees. He sheared 950 sheep. The helpers	49
that worked on this ranch said, "He is the fastest worker in the land."	63
Shelly did not get in shape. She said, "I am in shape. My	76
hands are fast. I have never been beaten in a shearing meet."	88
On the day of the meet, the tramp sat near the ranch gate. The	102
people from town came up the road. They waved to the tramp.	114
Then the people said, "We made bets that Shelly will beat	125
you." Then they went to the sheep shed and waited.	135
When Shelly came up the road, the people cheered. "Here's Shelly,"	146
they yelled.	148

> **A Note to the Parent**
>
> Listen to the student read the passage. Count the number of words read in one minute and the number of errors.
>
> Number of words read _____ Number of errors _____
>
> We read the story _____ times.
>
> (Parent's/Listener's) signature _____
>
> Date _____

Reading fluency

Part 1

Read the words in the box. Then fill in the blanks.

eat	slop	run	ran	slabs	see
fish	work	yellow	meat	pick	chomp
fresh	sleeve	meet	sheet	better	score

Chee had met a _____ dog in a _____ plant. The dog was named Rop, and he

_____ the plant. He said that he was _____ than Chee at doing things. Chee got

mad. So a _____ was set between Rop and Chee.

Rop said, "We will begin by seeing how fast we can _____."

Rop told a worker, "Get me 2 _____ of fresh meat."

Part 2

The words in the first column have endings.
Write the same words without endings in the second column.

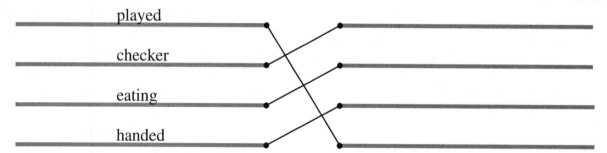

played

checker

eating

handed

Part 3

Copy the sentences:

She told the best joke.

_____

Chee began to stammer and say odd things.

_____

Vocabulary/context clues, inflectional suffixes, copying sentences

Part 4

Chee Meets Rop

Chee worked as a slate stacker for nearly a year. By then,	12
her rate of stacking was very good. But she was getting a little	25
sick of her job. "Stack, stack, stack," she said. "It's time	36
to do something else." So she went to the woman who ran the	49
slate plant and said, "I think I have to quit and get another job."	63
The woman said, "You have been a good worker. Good luck."	74
Chee left the plant and went looking for work. She came to a	87
sleeve plant. They made sleeves for coats in this plant.	98
Chee went into the plant and said to the people working in	111
a big room, "Where is the person who runs this plant?"	122
They went, "Ho, ho. We do not work for a person."	133
Chee told them, "You must work for someone. Show me who."	144
A man stepped up to Chee. The man said, "Step into that	156
room and you will see who runs this plant. His name is Rop."	169

> **A Note to the Parent**
>
> Listen to the student read the passage. Count the number of words read in one minute and the number of errors.
>
> Number of words read _____   Number of errors _____
>
> We read the story _____ times.
>
> (Parent's/Listener's) signature _____
>
> Date _____

Reading fluency

Part 1
Cross out the words that don't have **ea.**

rail	mean	hear	main	each	sleep
shear	began	these	tail	smell	beat
seating	real	pail	neck	between	reach

Part 2
Read the words in the box. Then fill in the blanks.

tricking	slapped	lap	sleeves	handed
stammer	making	slabs	slap	store
stabbed	coats	fast	score	wool

Chee and Rop went into the sleeve-_____ room of the plant. There Rop said, "I will get

the best _____ for this meet. We will see how fast that _____ dog can slap sleeves

in _____. The dog that slaps sleeves fastest will win."

Rop _____ Chee a needle. Chee went very fast, but she _____ herself with the

needle.

Part 3
The words in the first column have endings.
Write the same words without endings in the second column.

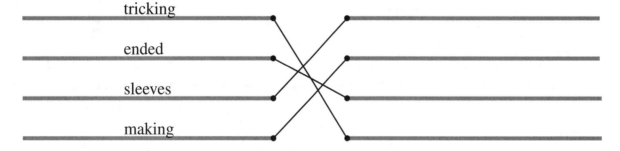

tricking

ended

sleeves

making

Sound/symbol correspondence, vocabulary/context clues, inflectional suffixes

Part 4

Rop and Chee Have a Meet

Chee had met a yellow dog in a sleeve plant. The yellow dog	13
was named Rop, and he ran the plant. He said that he was better	27
than Chee at doing things. Chee got mad. So a meet was set	40
between Rop and Chee. Rop said, "We will see if you can beat me	54
in this meet."	57
Rop yelled to the workers in the sleeve plant. "Stop sleeving	68
and get in here fast," he said. The workers ran into the room.	81
Rop said, "Chee and I are going to have a meet. We will begin by	96
seeing how fast we can eat."	102
Rop told a worker, "Get me 2 slabs of fresh meat. Drop the	115
slabs on the scale and see that they are the same."	126
A woman ran from the plant. She went to the store. She grabbed	139
2 slabs of meat that were on sale. She got back to the plant and	154
dropped them on the scale. Each slab was the same.	164

A Note to the Parent

Listen to the student read the passage. Count the number of words read in one minute and the number of errors.

Number of words read _____   Number of errors _____

We read the story _____ times.

(Parent's/Listener's) signature _____

Date _____

Reading fluency

Name _____

Part 1

The words in the first column have endings.
Write the same words without endings in the second column.

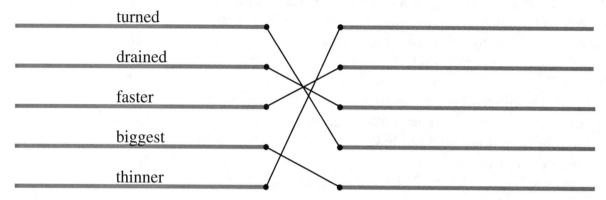

turned

drained

faster

biggest

thinner

Part 2

Write the words.

can + not = _____

any + body = _____

my + self = _____

some + one = _____

Part 3

Copy the sentences:

He sold gas at the boat ramp.

_____

She did not hear waves on the shore.

_____

Inflectional suffixes, compound words, copying sentences

Part 4

Sleeve Slapping

Chee and Rop went into the sleeve-making room of the plant.	11
There Rop said, "I will get the best score for this meet. We will see how fast	28
that lap dog can slap sleeves on coats. The dog that slaps sleeves	41
fastest will get the best score."	47
Rop handed Chee a needle. Rop said, "Take this needle and get	59
set to go. And don't stab yourself. Ho, ho."	68
Chee was mad. She held the needle and waited for Rop to say, "Go."	82
Rop said, "Get set. Go."	87
Chee went very fast, but she stabbed herself with the needle.	98
"Ow," she said.	101
"Ho, ho," Rop said. "That lap dog just stabbed herself. Ho, ho, ho,	114
hee, hee." As Rop was ho-heeing, he did not see where his needle	127
was going and he stabbed himself. "Ow," he said.	136
"Ho, hee, hep, hep, hep," Chee said.	143
Rop yelled, "Stop. This meet is over. I have slapped seven sleeves on coats.	157
So I am the champ, and I get the best score. Let's hear it for me."	173

A Note to the Parent

Listen to the student read the passage. Count the number of words read in one minute and the number of errors.

Number of words read _____   Number of errors _____

We read the story _____ times.

(Parent's/Listener's) signature _____

Date _____

Reading fluency

LESSON 39

Name _____

Part 1

Cross out the words that don't have **ee.**

steered	mean	hear	book	feel	sleep
cheer	began	these	sleeve	smell	beat
seating	wheel	deer	neck	between	steel

Part 2

Write the words.

any + one = _____

some + body = _____

her + self = _____

down + hill = _____

Part 3

Copy the sentences:

The boat was in the middle of the sea.

_____

The goat ate a hole in the boat.

_____

Part 4

The words in the first column have endings.
Write the same words without endings in the second column.

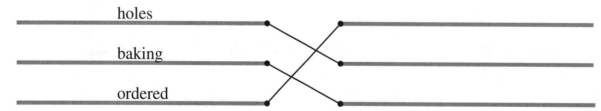

holes

baking

ordered

Sound/symbol correspondence, compound words, copying sentences, inflectional suffixes

Part 5

Sink That Ship

Kit made a boat. She made the boat of tin. The nose of the boat was	16
very thin. Kit said, "I think that this boat is ready for me to take on	32
the lake." So Kit went to the lake with her boat.	43
Her boat was a lot of fun. It went fast. But when she went to dock it	60
at the boat ramp, she did not slow it down. And the thin nose of the boat	77
cut a hole in the boat ramp.	84
The man who sold gas at the boat ramp got mad. He said, "That boat	99
cuts like a blade. Do not take the boat on this lake any more. Take	114
it where you will not run into things."	122
So Kit did not take her boat to the lake any more. She went to the sea	139
with her boat. She said, "There is a lot of room in the sea. I will not run	157
this boat into any docks."	162

A Note to the Parent   Listen to the student read the passage. Count the number of words read in one minute and the number of errors.

Number of words read _____   Number of errors _____

We read the story _____ times.

(Parent's/Listener's) signature _____

Date _____

Reading fluency

Part 1

The words in the first column have endings.
Write the same words without endings in the second column.

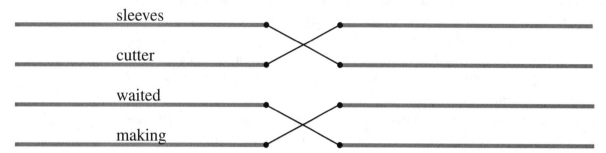

sleeves

cutter

waited

making

Part 2

Cross out the words that don't have **oa.**

goat	mean	boat	book	feel	loading
float	began	these	board	coat	beat

Part 3

Write the words.

an   +   other   =   _____

some +   one   =   _____

Part 4

Read the question and fill in the circle next to the answer. Write the answer in the blank.

1. Kit put rocks in the _____ of her boat.

   ○ back   ○ front   ○ top   ○ side

2. Kit said, "Things go fast when they go _____."

   ○ closer   ○ faster   ○ downhill   ○ through

3. The boat made a hole in the _____ of the bank.

   ○ back   ○ front   ○ slide   ○ side

Inflectional suffixes, sound/symbol correspondence, compound words, answering questions

68

Part 5

The Goat and Kit's Boat

Kit's boat was in the middle of the sea. It had made a hole in a	16
big ship. The big ship went down. Seventeen men, 47 women, three	28
dogs, and a pet goat got in Kit's boat. So Kit made holes in the bottom	44
of the boat to drain the water from the boat.	54
And the water did begin to drain, but not very fast. Kit said,	67
"These holes are not letting water out faster than the water is coming	80
in the boat. We need bigger holes."	91
A sailor said, "We left our tools on board the big ship, so we have	106
no way to make bigger holes."	112
A man said, "So let's just yell for help. HELP, HELP."	123
"Shut up," Kit said. "We will get back to shore if we just keep our	138
heads and think of a way to make a big hole that will drain water very fast."	155
An old woman said, "My pet goat likes to eat tin. Maybe he can	169
eat a hole in the bottom of this tin boat."	179

A Note to the Parent

Listen to the student read the passage. Count the number of words read in one minute and the number of errors.

Number of words read _____   Number of errors _____

We read the story _____ times.

(Parent's/Listener's) signature _____

Date _____

Reading fluency

Name _____

Part 1

Write the words.

good + bye = _____

no + thing = _____

any + body = _____

down + hill = _____

six + teen = _____

Part 2

Read the words in the box. Then fill in the blanks.

sail	boat	nobody	light	aim	white
bike	save	yellow	nothing	green	slow
red	sell	send	streak	pain	float

Kit said, "I am going to _____ this boat and get a _____. This boat is

_____ but a _____."

Then she said to herself, "I can have a lot of fun with a bike. If I get a _____ bike, it

will be very _____, so I'll fly over town."

Part 3

Cross out the words that don't have **ol.**

goat	told	boat	book	fold	loading
float	began	old	cold	meal	bolted

Compound words, vocabulary/context clues, sound/symbol correspondence

Part 4

Kit's Boat Goes Faster and Faster

This is another story about Kit and her tin boat. Kit had her boat at	16
the dock. She was fixing the hole that the goat made in the boat. She	30
painted her boat green. Then she asked the man who sold gas at the	44
dock, "Where can I get some big rocks?"	52
The man said, "Why do you need big rocks?"	61
Kit said, "I will drop them in the front of my boat."	73
The man asked, "Why will you do that?"	81
Kit said, "So that my boat will go faster. I don't like boats that go slow."	97
The man said, "How will the rocks in the front of your boat	110
make the boat go faster?"	115
Kit said, "Don't you see? The rocks will make the front of my boat	129
lower than the back of my boat. So my boat will be going downhill.	143
Things go very fast when they go downhill."	151
The man said, "Ho, ho. Those rocks will just make your boat go slower."	165

A Note to the Parent

Listen to the student read the passage. Count the number of words read in one minute and the number of errors.

Number of words read _____   Number of errors _____

We read the story _____ times.

(Parent's/Listener's) signature _____

Date _____

Reading fluency

Name _____

Part 1

Cross out the words that don't have **sh.**

shape	with	chest	shift	what
which	chop	fish	much	cheer

Part 2

The words in the first column have endings.
Write the same words without endings in the second column.

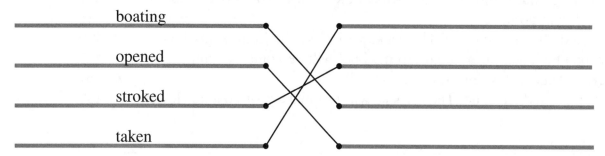

boating

opened

stroked

taken

Part 3

Write the words.

every + thing = _____

through + out = _____

good + bye = _____

with + out = _____

Part 4

Copy the sentences:

The shop man looked at the motor.

_____

She handed three books to him.

_____

Sound/symbol correspondence, inflectional suffixes, compound words, copying sentences

Part 5

Kit Makes Her Boat Lighter

Kit was in bad shape. She said, "I can fix things up."	12
The cop said, "Do not try to bribe us. This is a crime."	25
Kit said to her, "I was not trying to bribe you. But you must	39
help me. I need yellow paint."	45
The cop said, "Why do you need yellow paint?"	54
Kit said, "Get me the paint and you will see."	64
So the cop got another cop to run for the paint. The cop	77
stepped in front of Kit and said, "Do not try to leave." When	90
the other cop came back with the can of yellow paint, Kit smiled.	103
Then she took the lid from the can and began to paint her	116
boat yellow.	118
"What are you doing?" the cops asked. "How can it help	129
anything to paint that boat yellow?"	135
Kit grinned and said, "You will see."	142
Kit got in the boat, and the boat began to float up into the	156
sky. The cops said, "Do you see what I see? That boat is	169
floating in the sky."	173

> **A Note to the Parent**   Listen to the student read the passage. Count the number of words read in one minute and the number of errors.
>
> Number of words read _____   Number of errors _____
>
> We read the story _____ times.
>
> (Parent's/Listener's) signature _____
>
> Date _____

Reading fluency

Part 1

Write the words.

door　+　way　=　_____

home　+　work　=　_____

no　+　thing　=　_____

some　+　one　=　_____

Part 2

Cross out the words that don't have **ck.**

cash	packing	clapped	clocks	creek	trucker
rocked	neck	chops	milked	black	thinking

Part 3

Read the words in the box. Then fill in the blanks.

jumped	saw	bolts	tossed	mean	roar
tore	need	smiled	rod	grabbed	worker
fixed	whispered	motor	rubbed	reader	words

Molly said, "Here is the book. It tells where everything is on the _____. Read the book,

and it will tell you what you _____ to know."

So Molly went to the street and _____ into her hot rod. She _____ the wheel,

and she _____ down the street.

Henry took his book and _____ to himself, "I wish I was a better _____."

Compound words, sound/symbol correspondence, vocabulary/context clues

Part 4

Henry's Hot Rod

Henry had a hot rod. He ran his hot rod very fast down the freeway. But he	17
ran it too fast, and—wham!—there went his cam shaft. Henry said, "Now my	32
hot rod will not go."`	37
A truck came and dragged Henry's rod back to a motor shop. The shop	51
man looked at the motor. Then he rubbed his chin. He said, "I don't think	66
I can get to this job for three weeks. When do you need this heap?"	81
Henry said, "That hot rod is not a heap. Why can't you get to it now?"	97
The shop man rubbed his chin. Then he said, "I don't have time."	110
The shop man said, "I have three other jobs. When I get them fixed,	124
I can work on your hot rod."	131
Henry said, "Where can I take my hot rod to get it fixed now?"	145
The shop man said, "There is no shop in town that can do the work now.	161
They have lots of jobs."	166
"Why is that?" Henry asked.	171

A Note to the Parent

Listen to the student read the passage. Count the number of words read in one minute and the number of errors.

Number of words read _____   Number of errors _____

We read the story _____ times.

(Parent's/Listener's) signature _____

Date _____

Reading fluency

Part 1

The words in the first column have endings.
Write the same words without endings in the second column.

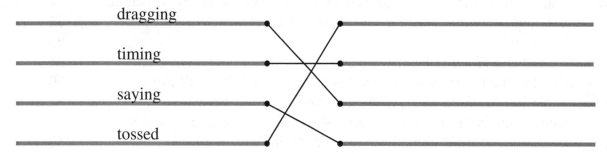

dragging

timing

saying

tossed

Part 2

Write the words.

some	+	body	=	_____
up	+	side	=	_____
with	+	out	=	_____
down	+	town	=	_____

Part 3

Read the question and fill in the circle next to the answer. Write the answer in the blank.

1. Henry was trying to fix a broken cam _____.

   ◯ shift   ◯ stick   ◯ shaft   ◯ stack

2. After a while, his motor was in little _____.

   ◯ gears   ◯ bits   ◯ rods   ◯ bolts

3. Molly fixed her hot rod because she was able to _____.

   ◯ work   ◯ know   ◯ bolt   ◯ read

Inflectional suffixes, compound words, vocabulary/context clues

Part 4

Henry's Sister Helps Him

Henry got a book on fixing motors. Henry went home with the	12
book. He sat in his hot rod and looked at the words in the book,	27
but Henry did not know how to read those words.	37
Here is what it said in the book: "There are three bolts that	50
hold this end of the cam shaft."	57
Here is what Henry was reading: "Where are there belts that	68
hold this end for a cam shaft."	75
Henry said, "What does that mean?"	81
He kept reading. Here is what it said in his book: "When you	94
take the seals from the shaft, you press on them and then lift	107
them from the shaft."	111
This is what Henry said when he was reading those words:	122
"Why take and steal I dress and then lifted them of the shaft."	135
Henry said, "I don't know what this book means." He tossed	146
the book down and said, "I don't need a book to fix this motor.	160
I have seen people work on motors, and I don't think it will be a very big job."	178

A Note to the Parent	Listen to the student read the passage. Count the number of words read in one minute and the number of errors.

Number of words read _____   Number of errors _____

We read the story _____ times.

(Parent's/Listener's) signature _____

Date _____

Reading fluency

Part 1

Write the words.

some   +   body   =   _____

up   +   set   =   _____

with   +   out   =   _____

door   +   way   =   _____

Part 2

The words in the first column have endings.
Write the same words without endings in the second column.

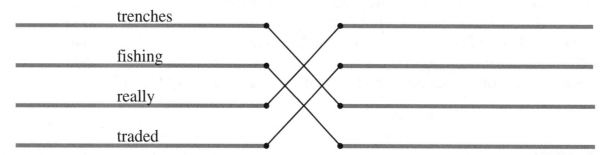

trenches

fishing

really

traded

Part 3

Read the words in the box. Then fill in the blanks.

rested	tires	sell	ripped	site	grip
crime	bikes	rid	roads	gripe	deal
conned	steal	ships	ready	paths	robbed

Kit said, "I think I will get _____ of this boat. It makes _____ sink. It has

_____ up 2 docks. It has made _____ and trenches. It tore holes in the bank, and

that is a bad _____."

Kit had a lot to _____ over. So she said, "I will _____ the boat."

Compound words, inflectional suffixes, vocabulary/context clues

Part 4

Molly Fixes Her Hot Rod

Henry was trying to fix his motor, but he was not doing	12
very well. He was looking at the words in his book on motors, but	26
Henry did not know what they said. The book said: "To turn a cam	40
shaft, you file each cam."	45
But this is what Henry said as he was reading: "To turn a cam	59
shaft, you fill each cam."	64
Henry said, "What does that mean?" He tossed the book aside	75
and said, "That book is not helping me very much. I can do the	89
job myself." So Henry worked and worked.	96
After a while, his motor was in little bits. Now he did not	109
have a motor. He had a heap of steel.	118
"Where is the cam shaft?" he asked as he looked at the big	131
pile of steel.	134
He picked up a big gear. "Is this a cam shaft?" he asked.	147
He ran his hand over the teeth of the gear. "These things must be cams," he said.	164
Henry was looking at the gear when a truck came down the street.	177
The truck was dragging his sister's hot rod.	185

A Note to the Parent

Listen to the student read the passage. Count the number of words read in one minute and the number of errors.

Number of words read _____   Number of errors _____

We read the story _____ times.

(Parent's/Listener's) signature _____

Date _____

Reading fluency

LESSON 46

Name _____

Part 1

Read the words in the box. Then fill in the blanks.

faster	really	lifted	ready	sold	worker
tires	fastest	robber	diver	zip	float
bikes	traded	back	pile	nose	slower

The con man had _____ his clock, his cash, his ring, and five _____ with holes

in them for Kit's tin boat.

Now the con man was _____ to become the best bank _____ in the west. He

said, "I will _____ rocks in the _____ of this boat. The more rocks I pile, the

_____ it will go."

Part 2

Match the words and complete them.

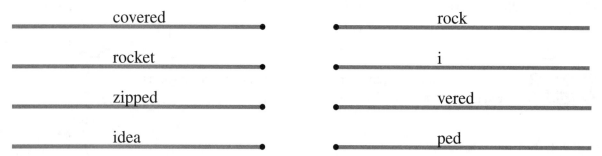

covered   rock

rocket   i

zipped   vered

idea   ped

Part 3

The words in the first column have endings.
Write the same words without endings in the second column.

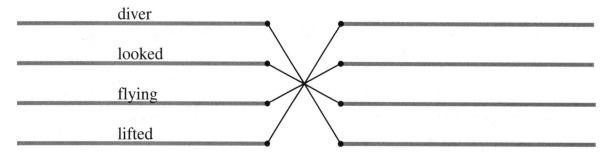

diver

looked

flying

lifted

Vocabulary/context clues, writing words, inflectional suffixes

80

Part 4

Kit's Trade

Kit said, "I think I will get rid of this boat. It makes	13
ships sink. It has ripped up 2 docks. It has made paths and	26
trenches. It tore holes in the bank, and that is a bad crime."	39
Kit had a lot to gripe over. So she said, "I will sell the	53
boat." She made a note and stuck it on the side of the tin boat.	68
The note said:	71
FOR SALE. A TIN BOAT	76
I WILL TRADE FOR A BIKE.	82
The con man was in town. He had five tires. Each tire had a	96
hole in it.	99
The con man said, "I will sit at this site until I see	112
someone to con." So he sat down on the tires. He was very tired.	126
While he rested, Kit came up the dock. The con man said to	139
himself, "If I can con this woman, I can get rid of my tires. Then I	155
will get some pike to eat. I like fish."	164
The con man said, "I have some fine tires if you have something to trade."	179

A Note to the Parent

Listen to the student read the passage. Count the number of words read in one minute and the number of errors.

Number of words read _____   Number of errors _____

We read the story _____ times.

(Parent's/Listener's) signature _____

Date _____

Reading fluency

Part 1

Write **1, 2,** or **3** in front of each sentence to show when these things happened in the story.
Then write the sentences in the blanks.

_____ The cops and their nine dogs ran up to the con man.

_____ The con man was sticking to the seat of the boat.

_____ The con man said, "This is a space ship, and I come from space."

1. _____

2. _____

3. _____

_____

Part 2

The words in the first column have endings.
Write the same words without endings in the second column.

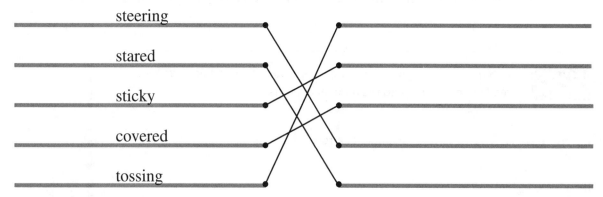

steering

stared

sticky

covered

tossing

Part 3

Copy the sentences:

She is the woman who runs the cotton mill.

_____

Slowly he began to stand up.

_____

Sequence, inflectional suffixes, copying sentences

Part 4

The Con Man Gets Cotton Taffy Pike

The con man had traded his clock, his cash, his ring, and	12
five tires with holes in them for Kit's tin boat.	22
Now the con man was ready to become the best bank robber in	35
the west. He said, "I will pile rocks in the nose of this boat.	49
The more rocks I pile, the faster it will go. So I will make this	64
boat the fastest thing there is."	70
So the con man slid the boat into deep water near the dock.	83
Then the con man got a big pile of rocks. He dropped ten rocks	97
into the nose of the boat. Then he dropped ten more.	108
He said, "Now this boat will go very fast." The nose of	120
the boat was low in the water.	127
The con man heaped ten more rocks into the nose of the boat.	140
Then he said, "Now this boat will sink." And it did. The	152
nose of the boat went down. And "glub, blub," the boat went to	165
the bottom of the sea.	170
The con man made a deal with a skin diver. The con man gave the	185
skin diver a coat.	189

▲ A Note to the Parent   Listen to the student read the passage. Count the number of words read in one minute and the number of errors.

Number of words read _____   Number of errors _____

We read the story _____ times.

(Parent's/Listener's) signature _____

Date _____

Reading fluency

Part 1

The words in the first column have endings.
Write the same words without endings in the second column.

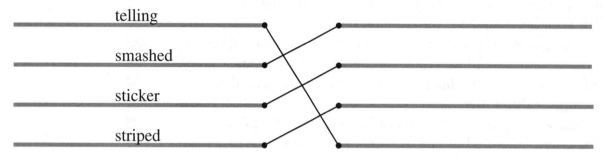

telling

smashed

sticker

striped

Part 2

Write the words.

boat   +   load   =   _____

home   +   work   =   _____

through +   out   =   _____

Part 3

Write **1, 2,** or **3** in front of each sentence to show when these things happened in the story.
Then write the sentences in the blanks.

_____ The con man began to run with the bags of gold, but he did not run very fast.

_____ The con man took bags of gold from the bank.

_____ The con man said, "I am from space, and I will get you."

1. _____

   _____

2. _____

   _____

3. _____

   _____

Inflectional suffixes, compound words, sequence

Part 4

A Thing from Space

The con man was zipping here and there in Kit's tin boat.	12
The boat went into a fish-packing plant, into a taffy plant, and	24
into a cotton mill. The con man was a mess. He had a mess of	39
cotton taffy pike in his boat. The steering wheel had taffy on it.	52
The con man said, "I must go somewhere and hide. I must throw	65
the rocks out of this boat so that it will slow down."	77
He began tossing cotton taffy rocks from the nose of the	88
boat. The boat went slower and slower. Then the con man began	100
heaving the pile of pike from the boat. Soon the main street of	113
the town had cotton taffy on it. The boat began to slow down.	126
The con man said, "Now I will run and hide before the cops	139
come here." But when he went to slip from the boat, he said,	152
"I am sticking to the seat. This taffy will not let go of me."	166
The cops and their nine dogs ran up to the con man. The man on	181
the dock ran up to him.	187

A Note to the Parent

Listen to the student read the passage. Count the number of words read in one minute and the number of errors.

Number of words read _____   Number of errors _____

We read the story _____ times.

(Parent's/Listener's) signature _____

Date _____

Reading fluency

Part 1

Write the word **trying.** Make a line over **ing.** _____

Write the word **moaned.** Make a line under **ed.** _____

Part 2

The words in the first column have endings.
Write the same words without endings in the second column.

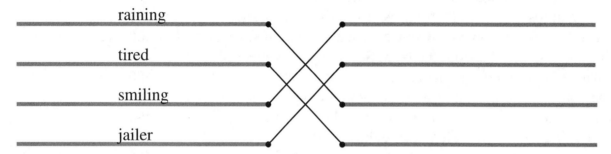

raining

tired

smiling

jailer

Part 3

Read the words in the box. Then fill in the blanks.

yelling	three	grain	seven	hair	pike
five	hard	slipped	rain	thing	leg
slapped	griping	drained	steps	trying	nose
raining	tired	light	jumped	drain	like

It was _____ and the con man was _____ about the _____. He said,

"My plan is going down the _____."

He was trying to run with _____ bags of gold, but they were not _____. He did

not run fast. The cotton in his _____ was running down his _____. He did not see

where he was going. He slipped in a pile of slippery _____ and fell down.

Part 4

Copy the sentence:

They began to lick the taffy.

Sound/symbol correspondence, inflectional suffixes, vocabulary/context clues, copying sentences

Part 5

The Bank Robbery Fails

The con man made everybody think that he was from space. He	12
was a big mass of cotton lint. The cotton lint was sticking to the	26
taffy. And the taffy was sticking to the con man's skin. It was	39
sticking to everything. The con man said to himself, "I will	50
give these people the scare of their lives."	58
He held up his hands and said a deep "Rrrrrr."	68
Three dogs went, "Ooooww," and ran down the street.	77
Then the con man said, "I am from space, and I will get you."	91
The dock man said, "I'm going to run to the sea and dive in."	105
That is what he did. So did the people from the plants.	117
The cops said, "Let's not make this space thing mad."	127
They smiled at him.	131
The con man said, "Rrrrrr. I will get you." He began to go for the cops.	147
The cops said, "We had better leave this spot." And they	158
did. They ran down the street and splash! They dived into the sea.	171
The con man was standing in the middle of	180
the street. Nobody was near him.	186

A Note to the Parent

Listen to the student read the passage. Count the number of words read in one minute and the number of errors.

Number of words read _____   Number of errors _____

We read the story _____ times.

(Parent's/Listener's) signature _____

Date _____

Reading fluency

LESSON 50

Name _____

Part 1

Write the word **digging.** Make a line over **ing.** _____

Write the word **lower.** Make a line under **er.** _____

Part 2

Write **1, 2,** or **3** in front of each sentence to show when these things happened in the story.
Then write the sentences in the blanks.

_____ The other bugs gave the dusty bug a dime to stay in the cool mine.

_____ The bugs went inside a big hole to be in a cool spot.

_____ The mother bug saw the dusty bug digging.

1. _____

_____

2. _____

_____

3. _____

_____

Part 3

The words in the first column have endings.
Write the same words without endings in the second column.

leaves

lower

hotter

walked

Sound/symbol correspondence, sequence, inflectional suffixes

Part 4

The Con Man Gets Busted

It was raining and the con man was griping about the rain.	12
He said, "My plan is going down the drain."	21
He was trying to run with the three bags of gold, but they	34
were not light and he did not run fast. The cotton in his hair	48
was running down his nose. He did not see where he was going. He	62
slipped on a pile of slippery pike and plop, plop, plop! The con man hit	77
the street, and the three bags of gold landed on the con man.	90
A little boy was standing near the con man. The boy said,	102
"You are not from space. I can see that you are just a wet man."	117
The lint was sliding from the con man's hair, from his hands,	129
from his nose, and from his coat. The rain was coming down very	142
fast, and the con man was very, very wet.	151
A dog ran up to the con man and began to lick the taffy from	166
his hand. "Don't bite me," the con man said. And the dog did not bite.	181
It licked and licked. It liked the taffy.	189

A Note to the Parent

Listen to the student read the passage. Count the number of words read in one minute and the number of errors.

Number of words read _____   Number of errors _____

We read the story _____ times.

(Parent's/Listener's) signature _____

Date _____

Reading fluency

Part 1

Read the question and fill in the circle next to the answer. Write the answer in the blank.

1. The dusty bug liked _____.

   ○ bills   ○ shovels   ○ dills   ○ smells

2. The bug said, "I don't have _____ with me."

   ○ pickles   ○ cash   ○ tubs   ○ mine

3. The bug dug into the _____ and got a big pickle.

   ○ store   ○ bag   ○ mine   ○ tub

Part 2

Write the word **outside.** Make a line over **out.** _____

Write the word **another.** Make a line under **er.** _____

Part 3
Match the words and complete them.

joking		gri
rotten		cl
clerk		king
grinned		ten

Part 4
Copy this sentence.

The dusty bug smiled from the door of the store.

_____

Vocabulary/context clues, sound/symbol correspondence, inflectional suffixes, copying sentences

Part 5

The Bug That Dug

There was a bug. That bug liked to dig. He dug and dug. His	14
mother said, "Why do you keep digging? The rest of us bugs eat	27
leaves and sit in the shade. But you dig and dig."	38
"When I dig, I feel happy," the digging bug said. "I like	50
to make holes."	53
So he made holes. When he stopped digging, he was dusty. His	65
brothers and sisters said, "You are a mess. You have dust on	77
your back. What are you doing?"	83
The bug said, "When I dig, I feel happy." And so that bug	96
dug and dug.	99
Then something happened. The days began to get hotter and	109
hotter. The sun was so hot that the other bugs said, "We cannot	122
stay here. It is too hot. We must go to a spot that is not so hot."	139
They walked here and there, but they did not find a spot that	152
felt cool. Then they came to a big hole in the side of a hill. They said,	169
"Let's go down this hole. It looks cool inside."	178
The bugs went inside the hole.	184

A Note to the Parent

Listen to the student read the passage. Count the number of words read in one minute and the number of errors.

Number of words read _____   Number of errors _____

We read the story _____ times.

(Parent's/Listener's) signature _____

Date _____

Reading fluency

Part 1
Match the words and complete them.

orange ●   ● man

holding ●   ● hold

drink ●   ● or

woman ●   ● dr

Part 2
Read the words in the box. Then fill in the blanks.

table	grabbed	stopped	bib	fixed	binging
taken	broken	dropped	cheer	deer	door
dropping	floor	fixing	making	sound	leak

The clock maker _____ the clock and _____ it. The clock made a loud

_____ when it hit the _____. The _____ fell out. A spring went, "bop."

The clock went, "bing, bing, ding."

The clock maker said, "That clock is _____. Let me make a bid on _____ it."

Part 3
Write the words.

ding   +   ing   =   _____

real   +   ly   =   _____

sleep   +   ing   =   _____

loud   +   ly   =   _____

Writing words, vocabulary/context clues, inflectional/derivational suffixes

© SRA/McGraw-Hill. Permission is granted to reproduce for classroom use.

Name _____

Part 4

The Bug and the Pickle Tub

The dusty bug was resting in his mine. It was hot outside.	12
He had a rusty shovel. He had been digging with the shovel, but	25
now he was tired. He said, "I need to eat. I like dill pickles,	39
but I don't have any dills."	45
He tossed the shovel to one side. Then he came out of his	58
mine. The sun was very hot. The bug went to a store. Then he	72
picked up a tub of pickles. He said to the clerk, "Will you bill	86
me for these dill pickles?"	91
The clerk said, "No, we do not bill for pickles. You must pay	104
cash in this store."	108
The bug said, "I don't have cash with me. But if you send	121
me a bill, I will pay for it."	129
The clerk said, "You did not hear me. I said that we do not	143
bill for dill pickles."	147
The bug said, "That's fine with me. Now that I smell these	159
pickles, I can tell that they are rotten."	167
"They are not rotten," the clerk said. "They are the best	178
pickles in town."	181

A Note to the Parent

Listen to the student read the passage. Count the number of words read in one minute and the number of errors.

Number of words read _____   Number of errors _____

We read the story _____ times.

(Parent's/Listener's) signature _____

Date _____

Reading fluency

Part 1

Write **1, 2,** or **3** in front of each sentence to show when these things happened in the story. Then write the sentences in the blanks.

_____ The clock maker slapped a bell into the deer clock.

_____ The clock maker painted the deer yellow.

_____ The woman tossed the clock down, and it broke into parts.

1. _____

2. _____

3. _____

   _____

Part 2

The words in the first column have endings.
Write the same words without endings in the second column.

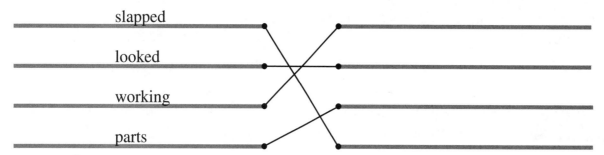

slapped

looked

working

parts

Part 3

Write the word **himself.** Make a line over **self.** _____

Write the word **dabbed.** Make a line under **ed.** _____

Part 4

Copy this sentence.

A woman was standing near the door.

_____

Sequence, inflectional suffixes, sound/symbol correspondence, copying sentences

Part 4

The Old Clock Maker

The old clock maker liked to work with plants when he	11
wasn't working with clocks. He had lots of plants in back of his	24
home. Every day after work, he dressed in a bib and went to	37
dabble with his plants. While he dabbled, he talked. He didn't	48
hear himself, so he didn't know that he was saying things very	60
loudly. When he came to a plant that did not have buds, he said,	74
"This plant is a dud, because it doesn't have one bud."	85
One day, he was dabbling and talking when his wife came	96
out. She said, "A woman is here. Can you make a bid on fixing a clock?"	112
The old clock maker did not hear her. The clock maker said,	124
"I do not have a rip in my bib."	133
His wife said, "I did not say 'bib,' I said 'bid.' A woman	146
needs a bid. Can you tell her how much she will have to pay?"	160
"I'm not going to the bay," the clock maker said. "I'm	171
going to stay here with the bees and my plants."	181

> **A Note to the Parent**
>
> Listen to the student read the passage. Count the number of words read in one minute and the number of errors.
>
> Number of words read _____　Number of errors _____
>
> We read the story _____ times.
>
> (Parent's/Listener's) signature _____
>
> Date _____

Reading fluency

Name _____

Part 1

Write the words.

every + thing = _____

with + out = _____

door + way = _____

out + side = _____

Part 2

Write **1, 2,** or **3** in front of each sentence to show when these things happened in the story.
Then write the sentences in the blanks.

_____ The old clock maker took the clock back to the woman.

_____ An alligator ran across the front of the clock and bit the clock maker's finger.

_____ The clock maker stuck antlers on the alligator and slapped it into the deer clock.

1. _____

_____

2. _____

_____

3. _____

_____

Part 3

The words in the first column have endings.
Write the same words without endings in the second column.

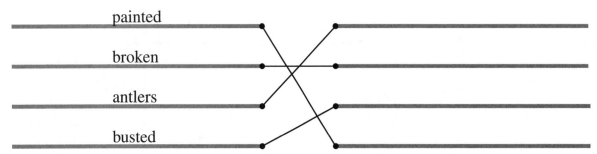

painted

broken

antlers

busted

Compound words, sequence, inflectional suffixes

96

Part 4

The Deer That Bobbed Like a Frog

The clock maker gave a bid on the clock that he had	12
dropped. He made a bid of eleven dollars. Then he took the clock	25
to his work room. In that room he had lots of clocks. Every hour,	39
the clocks went, "dong, dong" and "ding, ding." But the clock	50
maker did not hear them.	55
In the work room, the clock maker had a bin of parts from	68
other clocks. He also had a lot of tools for fixing clocks.	80
The clock maker held the clock with the deer. He said, "I	92
will have to paint this clock." So he got a brush and dabbed	105
paint on the clock.	109
He made the clock orange. Then he dabbed paint on the deer.	121
He made the deer yellow.	126
Then he went to his bin of old clocks to look for one that had	141
a good deer. He looked and looked. Then he began to talk to	154
himself. He said, "This is bad. I made a bid on fixing this	167
clock, but I cannot see another clock with a working deer. The best	180
I can see is a clock with a working frog."	190

A Note to the Parent

Listen to the student read the passage. Count the number of words read in one minute and the number of errors.

Number of words read _____   Number of errors _____

We read the story _____ times.

(Parent's/Listener's) signature _____

Date _____

Reading fluency

Part 1

Copy the sentences.

The woman tossed the clock into a tree.

_____

A little yellow bird sat on the alligator's antlers.

_____

Part 2

The words in the first column have endings.
Write the same words without endings in the second column.

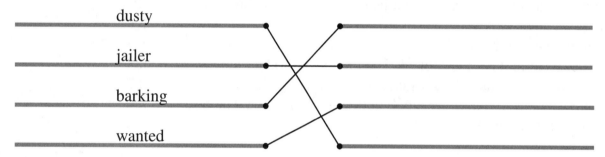

dusty

jailer

barking

wanted

Part 3

Read the words in the box. Then fill in the blanks.

third	home	first	next	stayed	way
leaves	time	came	come	bees	house
pay	play	buy	days	birds	trees

The woman said, "For some _____, I've wanted to get those _____ into my

tree, but this is the _____ time they've _____ to the tree. Thank you. How can I

_____ you?"

"Hand me eleven dollars, and I'll be on my _____ this day," the clock maker said. So

the woman gave the clock maker eleven dollars, and he went _____.

Name _____

Part 4

An Alligator Clock

The clock maker had painted a clock orange. He had made the	12
deer yellow. He had fixed the deer so that it bobbed up and down	26
like a frog. When the clock maker took the clock to the woman,	39
the woman got very mad. She tossed the clock down. The clock	51
maker took the broken clock back to his shop. He was going to fix it again.	67
He had just put his work bib on when his wife came in. She	81
said, "Did you just come in?"	87
"Yes," the clock maker said, "I can grin." And he did.	98
His wife shook her head. Then she said, "A little girl is	110
outside. She wants to know if she can pick weeds in your garden."	123
The clock maker said, "There are no seeds in my garden.	134
The plants are just getting buds. They won't have seeds before	145
the end of summer."	149
"Not seeds," his wife said: "Weeds. The girl wants to pick weeds."	161
"Why does she want to plant weeds?" the clock maker asked.	172
His wife was getting mad. She said, "I will tell her that she	185
can pick weeds."	188

> **A Note to the Parent**
>
> Listen to the student read the passage. Count the number of words read in one minute and the number of errors.
>
> Number of words read _____   Number of errors _____
>
> We read the story _____ times.
>
> (Parent's/Listener's) signature _____
>
> Date _____

Reading fluency

Part 1

Write **1, 2,** or **3** in front of each sentence to show when these things happened in the story.
Then write the sentences in the blanks.

_____ The doctor said, "Lock this man up."

_____ The bus took the con man to the rest home.

_____ The con man got down on the floor and growled at the nurse.

1. _____

_____

2. _____

3. _____

Part 2

The words in the first column have endings.
Write the same words without endings in the second column.

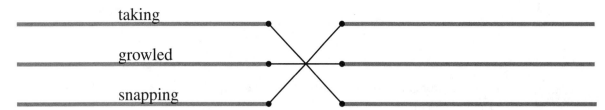

taking

growled

snapping

Part 3

Match the words and complete them.

pretty   dow

window   gar

garden   pre

Part 4

Write the words.

out   +   side   =   _____

him   +   self   =   _____

Sequence, inflectional suffixes, writing words, compound words

Part 4

The Clock in the Tree

The clock maker had taken an alligator from a dusty old	11
clock and had slapped it into the deer clock. The alligator was	23
yellow, and it had antlers. The old man said, "This clock looks	35
just like it did before."	40
So the clock maker took the clock to the woman. The clock	52
maker rapped on her door. The woman came to the door. "What do	65
you want?" she said.	69
"Here it is," the clock maker said. He held up the alligator	81
clock. "This clock is fixed up as good as ever."	91
The woman looked at the clock and said, "Oh, no. I don't	103
want to buy dusty clocks with beads on them. I had a good clock,	117
and you busted that clock. Now you are selling old junk clocks."	129
"Yes," the old clock maker said. "It looks just as good as	141
ever. Here, hold it while I set the hands."	150
Before the woman was able to back away, the clock maker handed	162
her the clock and began to set the hands. As soon as the hands were	177
set for five o'clock, the clock made a loud sound. "Blip, blop,"	189
sounded the bell.	192

> **A Note to the Parent**
>
> Listen to the student read the passage. Count the number of words read in one minute and the number of errors.
>
> Number of words read _____   Number of errors _____
>
> We read the story _____ times.
>
> (Parent's/Listener's) signature _____
>
> Date _____

Reading fluency

Name _____

Part 1

Write the words.

be + fore = _____

some + where = _____

any + one = _____

your + self = _____

Part 2

Copy the sentences.

He tried to get out the window.

_____

They looked around and didn't see anybody.

_____

The doctor took notes on a pad.

_____

Part 3

Write the name of the person each sentence tells about.

president   con man

1. This person had to be a private in the army.   _____

2. This person said, "You must do everything I say."   _____

3. This person marched and marched and marched.   _____

Compound words, copying sentences, characterization

Part 4

The Con Man Acts Like a Dog

When we left the con man, he was in the hospital. He had	13
told the cops and the jailer that he was sick. He really wasn't	26
sick. He was just playing sick. But the cop took him to the	39
hospital. The cop went up to a nurse and said, "Nurse, I have a	53
sick man. He needs help."	58
The nurse said, "We will fix him up fast." She had the con	71
man sit on a cart. Then she took the con man to a room.	85
As soon as she left the room, the con man darted for the door.	99
He peeked outside. But the cop was standing near the door.	110
"Nuts," the con man said. "I will try the window."	120
He darted to the window. He grabbed the handles and opened	131
it wide. Then he looked out. There were bars on the window.	143
"Nuts," the con man said.	148
He sat on the bed and said to himself, "I must think of a	162
trick that will get me out of here." Suddenly he jumped up.	174
"I've got it," he yelled. Then he began to bark like a dog.	187
He had a plan.	191

A Note to the Parent

Listen to the student read the passage. Count the number of words read in one minute and the number of errors.

Number of words read _____   Number of errors _____

We read the story _____ times.

(Parent's/Listener's) signature _____

Date _____

Reading fluency

Part 1

Write the word **wheat.** Make a line under **ea.**   _____

Write the word **hiding.** Make a line over **ing.**   _____

Part 2

The words in the first column have endings.
Write the same words without endings in the second column.

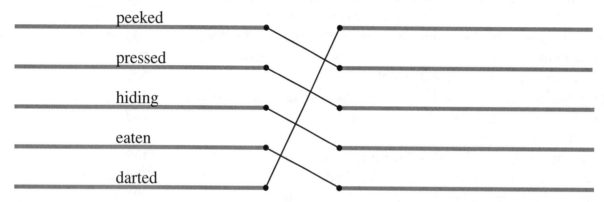

peeked

pressed

hiding

eaten

darted

Part 3

Write **1, 2,** or **3** in front of each sentence to show when these things happened in the story.
Then write the sentences in the blanks.

_____ The president began to scream, "Oh, my foot. It is stuck in the gate."

_____ The con man and the president hid under the bed.

_____ The man who ran the gate pressed the button and the gate opened.

1. _____

2. _____

_____

3. _____

_____

Part 4

The Con Man Meets the President

The con man had told the doctor that he was very foxy. The	13
doctor had two helpers lock up the con man. The doctor said,	25
"That man thinks he's a fox now."	32
So the helpers took the con man to a little room at the far	46
end of the yard. They said, "You will like this room. You will	59
have a good time."	63
The con man said, "I am too smart for you. I will get out of	78
this room before the sun sets."	84
But the sun set, and the con man hadn't found a way to get out	99
of the room. He pounded on the floor. He tried to get out the	113
window. But the window had bars on it. And the bars did not bend.	127
At last, the con man sat down on the bed. He said, "I will	141
have to think with my brains. There must be some way to get out of here."	157
Somebody said, "It is easy to get out of here."	167
The con man looked around the room, but he did not see anybody.	180
The con man said, "Maybe I am out of it. I am hearing people talk."	195

A Note to the Parent

Listen to the student read the passage. Count the number of words read in one minute and the number of errors.

Number of words read _____   Number of errors _____

We read the story _____ times.

(Parent's/Listener's) signature _____

Date _____

Reading fluency

Part 1

Write the words.

near   +   by   =   _____

with   +   out   =   _____

be   +   cause   =   _____

loud   +   ly   =   _____

Part 2

Write **1, 2,** or **3** in front of each sentence to show when these things happened in the story.
Then write the sentences in the blanks.

_____ The president said very loudly, "We are from the bug company."

_____ The woman in the main office said, "Take the green car in front of the office."

_____ The con man and the president dressed in white jackets and left the shack.

1. _____

_____

2. _____

_____

3. _____

_____

Part 3

The words in the first column have endings.
Write the same words without endings in the second column.

_____ steered _____

_____ nearest _____

_____ stared _____

Compound words, sequence, inflectional/derivational suffixes

Part 4

A Foxy Escape, Part 1

The con man was in a room with a man who said that he was	15
President Washington. President Washington said that he was in	24
charge of their escape. The con man was just a private in his army.	38
The next day, the president said, "Soon they will come around	49
to feed us. When we hear them at the door, we will zip under the	64
bed. And we will wait without making a sound. Remember to do	76
everything I say, because I don't want anything to mar my plans."	88
"Yes, sir," the con man said. He was very tired. He had	100
marched and marched. He had taken lots of orders from the president.	112
Just then, there was a sound outside the door. "Quick," the president	124
said. "Dart under the bed. And don't let your feet show."	135
The con man darted under the bed. The president darted under	146
the bed. Then the president whispered, "There is dust under this	157
bed, and dust makes me sneeze."	163
The con man whispered, "Don't sneeze."	169
"Shut up, private," whispered the president.	175
The door opened. The con man peeked out and saw two legs walking	188
across the room.	191

A Note to the Parent

Listen to the student read the passage. Count the number of words read in one minute and the number of errors.

Number of words read _____   Number of errors _____

We read the story _____ times.

(Parent's/Listener's) signature _____

Date _____

Reading fluency

Part 1

Cross out the words that don't have **ar.**

chair	alarm	about	drain	started	talking
army	scream	darted	charge	track	sharp

Part 2

Write the name of the person each sentence tells about.

president   **con man**

1. This person said, "I need something to eat." _____

2. This person ordered a big lunch for two. _____

3. This person said, "I must get away from this guy." _____

4. This person rolled right off the side of the bed. _____

5. This person said, "Just charge it to the room." _____

6. This person smiled and said, "Tee, hee." _____

Part 3

The words in the first column have endings. Write the same words without endings in the second column.

suddenly

rapped

snoring

shaved

Part 4

A Foxy Escape, Part 2

The con man ran from the grove of trees. He jogged up to	13
the president. The president smiled and said, "You see, private,	23
the gate is open. And we are free. Let's run down that road	36
before these yokels come after us."	42

So the con man and the president ran down the road. The people 55
from the rest home ran up to the gate. They said to the gate man, 70
"Did you open the gate and let those men escape?" 80

"Yes, I did," the gate man said. "But the first man had his 93
foot stuck in the gate. He was in pain." 102

"You yokel," the people said. Six people began to run after 113
the con man and the president. 119

"I'm getting tired," the con man said. "Let's stop and rest." 130

"Shut up, private," the president said. "You'll never 138
become a major thinking the way you do." 146

"I don't want to become a major," the con man said. "I just 159
want to get out of here." 165

"Then do what I say," the president shouted. "We're going back to 177
the rest home. Follow me." 182

"What?" the con man asked. "We can't go back. They'll get us." 194

A Note to the Parent   Listen to the student read the passage. Count the number of words read in one minute and the number of errors.

Number of words read _____   Number of errors _____

We read the story _____ times.

(Parent's/Listener's) signature _____

Date _____

Reading fluency

Name _____

Part 1

Write the word **hamburger.** Make a line over **er.** _____

Write the word **please.** Make a line under **ea.** _____

Part 2

Write **1, 2,** or **3** in front of each sentence to show when these things happened in the story. Then write the sentences in the blanks.

_____ The president said to the man behind the desk, "Give me my money back."

_____ The president cut some hair from the man's wig and made a beard with it.

_____ The president and the con man got into a cab and drove away.

1. _____

_____

2. _____

_____

3. _____

_____

Part 3

Write the name of the person each sentence tells about.

president   con man   man at the desk

1. This person began to tell a story about a battle. _____

2. This person said, "We must escape." _____

3. This person said, "Well, let's dash, buster." _____

4. This person said that there were bugs in the hotel. _____

5. This person handed over two hundred dollars. _____

Sound/symbol correspondence, sequence, characterization

Name _____

Part 4

The Con Man Becomes a Bride

The president and the con man were in the bridal rooms of a	13
big hotel. The president had told the man at the desk that he and	27
the con man were from the bug company. The president had said	39
that somebody called about the bugs in the bridal rooms.	49
The president said, "This is the life." He sat down on the	61
bed. "I need something to eat, private. Go down to the dining	73
room and get a big lunch for us. Charge it to the room."	86
The con man said, "But I'm not—"	93
"Hush up, private," the president yelled. "If you want to	103
stay in this army, you must remember that I am in charge."	115
"Yes, sir," the con man said.	121
The con man went down to the dining room and ordered a big	134
lunch for two. "Charge it to the bridal rooms," he said.	145
Then he went back to the bridal rooms. The president was	156
sleeping on the bed. The con man said to himself, "I must get	169
away from this guy, but I need a plan."	178
He sat in the chair and began to think.	187

A Note to the Parent

Listen to the student read the passage. Count the number of words read in one minute and the number of errors.

Number of words read _____   Number of errors _____

We read the story _____ times.

(Parent's/Listener's) signature _____

Date _____

Reading fluency

Part 1

The words in the first column have endings.
Write the same words without endings in the second column.

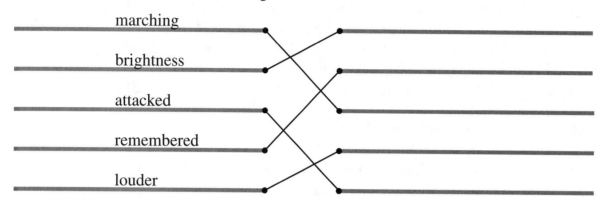

marching

brightness

attacked

remembered

louder

Part 2

Read the question and fill in the circle next to the answer. Write the answer in the blank.

1. Jean was on night _____ in this story.

   ○ planet   ○ play   ○ march   ○ patrol

2. There were _____ moons in the night sky.

   ○ three   ○ five   ○ third   ○ six

3. The drams moved like a big _____ when they came out of the lake.

   ○ army   ○ patrol   ○ grasshopper   ○ enemy

4. The drams would _____ everything in their path.

   ○ stop   ○ eat   ○ reach   ○ wake

Part 3

Write the words.

grass   +   hopper =   _____

spot   +   light   =   _____

some   +   thing   =   _____

Inflectional/derivational suffixes, vocabulary/context clues, compound words

Part 4

The Escape from the Hotel

The con man and the president were having lunch in the	11
bridal room. The president said, "This room is a mess. I told	23
that bum private to get lunch. But look at the junk he ordered.	36
Hamburgers and cake. The army just isn't what it was years ago."	48
The con man said, "You are so right."	56
"Yes, my dear. Let me tell you about the battle that we had	69
some years back. The enemy army had us holed up in a spot named	83
Valley Forge. We were—"	87
Suddenly, the president stopped. He jumped up and sniffed the	97
air. "I smell the enemy," he said. "They are going to attack. I	110
know it. And I don't even have my army with me. Where is that private?"	125
The president ran to the window and looked down at the	136
street. "There are cop cars down there. We must escape."	146
The president ran to the closet and came back with dress pants	158
and a striped coat. He slipped into them. Then he cut some hair	171
from the con man's wig and made a beard with it. He stuck the	185
beard on his chin.	189

📖 A Note to the Parent   Listen to the student read the passage. Count the number of words read in one minute and the number of errors.

Number of words read _____   Number of errors _____

We read the story _____ times.

(Parent's/Listener's) signature _____

Date _____

Reading fluency

Name _____

Part 1

Write the words.

her   +   self   = _____

what   +   ever   = _____

moon   +   light   = _____

some   +   body   = _____

Part 2

Read the words in the box. Then fill in the blanks.

reached	far	shirt	closer	light	signaler
skipped	inches	drams	pocket	pressed	springs
frozen	barracks	messed	meters	melted	stabbed

Jean couldn't seem to move. She stared at the drams as they came _____. They were

only a few _____ from her now.

"Move," she said to herself. But her legs felt as if they had _____.

Then Jean began to think. She _____ for her _____. She _____

the button. Lights began to flash in the _____. Women began to yell, "The drams! The

drams! Let's get out of here."

And Jean began to run. Now her legs felt like _____. Did she ever run!

Part 3

Copy the sentence.

Suddenly, a sound came from the other room.

_____

_____

Compound words, vocabulary/context clues, copying sentences

Part 4

Jean on Patrol

The night was cool. Jean looked up at the five moons in the	13
night sky. "I will never feel at home on this planet," she said	26
to herself. She was on night patrol. Her job was to patrol a	39
strip that led from the beach of the red lake to the barracks.	52
Nobody liked night patrol, not with the drams.	60
The drams were little animals that lived in the red lake. They	72
looked like grasshoppers, but they were bigger. About three times	82
a year, they came out of the lake. When they did, things got very	96
bad. They ate everything in their path. They ate wood and bricks.	108
They ate the yellow plants that lived on the planet.	118
Last year, they had eaten the barracks. Seven years before	128
that, they had attacked some of the women who didn't get out of	141
the barracks. Nobody could find a way to stop them. The drams	153
moved like a big army, with millions and millions of drams	164
marching and eating, marching and eating.	170
Jean had been on the planet for a little more than six months.	183
She had seen the drams before.	189

A Note to the Parent

Listen to the student read the passage. Count the number of words read in one minute and the number of errors.

Number of words read _____   Number of errors _____

We read the story _____ times.

(Parent's/Listener's) signature _____

Date _____

Reading fluency

Part 1

The words in the first column have endings.
Write the same words without endings in the second column.

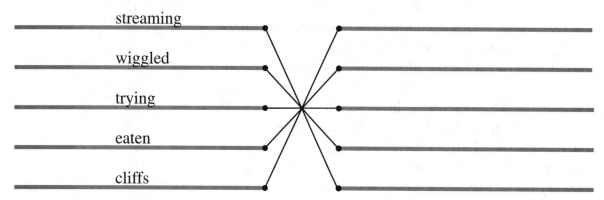

streaming

wiggled

trying

eaten

cliffs

Part 2

Write **1, 2,** or **3** in front of each sentence to show the order that these things happened in the story.

_____ Two women held Jean while the others slapped the drams.

_____ There was a mass of drams on Jean.

_____ Jean found out that Carla was on patrol.

Part 3

Write the name of the person each sentence tells about.

    Jean   Carla   major

1. This person was not in her room.   _____

2. This person made a loud sound with the trumpet.   _____

3. This person wiggled and tried to shake off the drams.   _____

4. This person fell into a hole in the floor of the barracks.   _____

5. This person was on patrol near the cliffs.   _____

6. This person said, "You did a brave thing."   _____

Inflectional suffixes, sequence, characterization

Name _____

Part 4

The Drams Attack

For a moment, Jean was frozen as she looked at the drams	12
coming from the lake. She could see them clearly in the	23
moonlight. They were shiny as they moved up the beach.	33
For a moment, Jean didn't remember that she was to signal the	45
barracks as soon as she spotted drams. She wanted to run—run	57
as fast as she could go. She wanted to run as far from the drams	72
as she could get. But she couldn't seem to move. She stared at	85
the drams as they came closer and closer. They were only a few	98
meters from her now.	102
"Move. Get out of here," she said to herself. But her	113
legs felt as if they had melted.	120
Then Jean began to think. She reached for her signaler. She	131
pressed the button. Lights began to flash in the barracks. Women	142
began to yell, "The drams! The drams! Let's get out of here."	154
And Jean began to run. Now her legs felt like springs. Did she	167
ever run! It was about three blocks from the beach to the	179
barracks, and Jean ran to the barracks so fast that she felt as	192
if she had run only a few meters.	200

A Note to the Parent

Listen to the student read the passage. Count the number of words read in one minute and the number of errors.

Number of words read _____   Number of errors _____

We read the story _____ times.

(Parent's/Listener's) signature _____

Date _____

Reading fluency

Part 1

Write **1**, **2**, or **3** in front of each sentence to show the order that these things happened in the story.

_____ Jean tried to think of everthing that happened just before the drams went to sleep.

_____ The major told the others why the trumpet made the drams sleep.

_____ Jean gave a blast on Carla's trumpet.

Part 2

The words in the first column have endings.
Write the same words without endings in the second column.

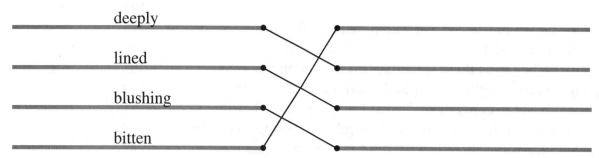

deeply

lined

blushing

bitten

Part 3

Read the words in the box. Then fill in the blanks.

barracks	bubbles	blushed	sound	fill	smiled
animals	horns	hunger	felt	showed	leave
line	march	patrol	water	hungry	blast

One of the women said, "Does that mean that we can stop the drams just by blowing

_____ when they come out of the _____?"

"We can do better than that," the major said. "We can pipe _____ into the lake. We can

keep them from getting _____ for sound. Then they won't _____ the lake."

The women _____ and looked at each other. Jean was thinking, "Now night

_____ won't be so bad."

Part 4

Trapped in the Barracks

The drams were at the other end of the barracks. They had	12
eaten the wall, and now they were streaming over the floor. Jean	24
was standing outside the door to Carla's room. Carla was not in	36
sight. Jean had to get out of the barracks before the drams	48
reached her. And she had to find Carla. The drams were coming	60
closer. The "bzzzzzz" was very loud.	66
Jean ran into Carla's room. She grabbed the trumpet from	76
Carla's table. "I can make a loud sound with this horn," Jean	98
said to herself. She took in a lot of air. Then she pressed the	112
trumpet to her lips.	116
"Brrrrrooooooooooooo," went the horn.	120
Suddenly the floor shifted. A crash came from the middle of	131
the barracks. The drams were getting closer. "No time to blow	142
the horn again," Jean said to herself. "I must get out of here."	155
She ran from Carla's room. A mass of drams was on the floor.	168
Jean tried to run past them, but one dram got on her leg. It bit	183
a hole in her pants. Jean tried to slap it off, and she tried to run	199
at the same time.	203

A Note to the Parent

Listen to the student read the passage. Count the number of words read in one minute and the number of errors.

Number of words read _____   Number of errors _____

We read the story _____ times.

(Parent's/Listener's) signature _____

Date _____

Reading fluency

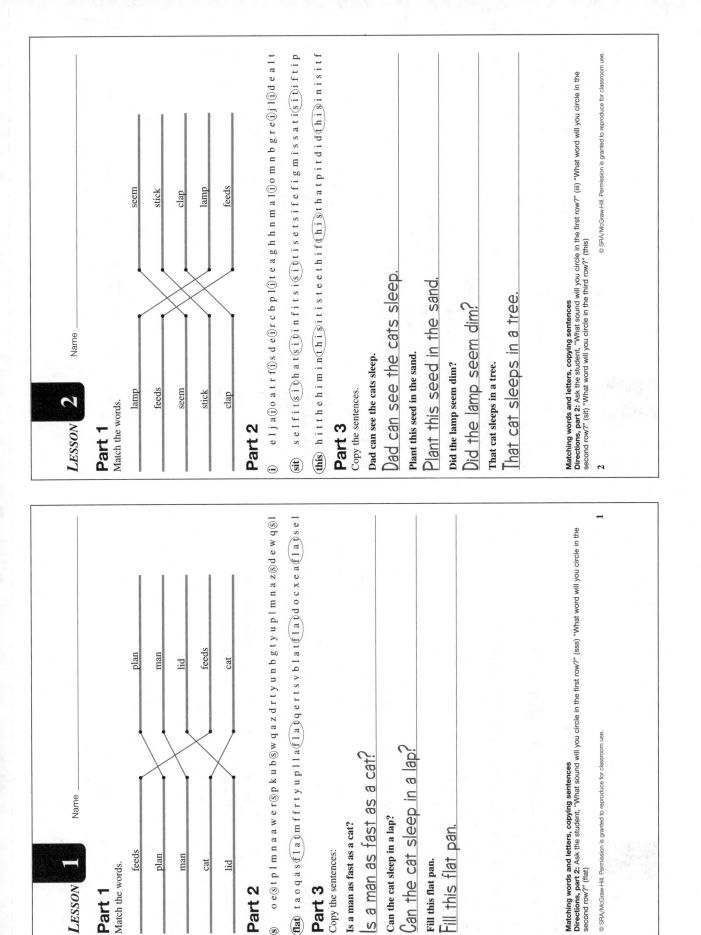

LESSON 1

Name _____

Part 1
Match the words.

feeds — plan
plan — man
man — lid
cat — feeds
lid — cat

Part 2

(s) o e (s) t p l m n a a w e r (s) p k u b (s) w q a z d r t y u n b g t y u p l m n a z (s) d e w q (s) l

(flat) t a o q a s (flat) m f f r t y u p l l a (flat) q e r t s v b l a t (flat) d o c x e a (flat) s e l

Part 3
Copy the sentences:

Is a man as fast as a cat?

Is a man as fast as a cat?

Can the cat sleep in a lap?

Can the cat sleep in a lap?

Fill this flat pan.

Fill this flat pan.

1

LESSON 2

Name _____

Part 1
Match the words.

lamp — seem
feeds — stick
seem — clap
stick — lamp
clap — feeds

Part 2

(i) e l j a (i) o a t r f (i) s d e (i) r c b p l (i) t e a g h h n m a l (i) o m n b g r e (i) j l (i) d e a l t

(sit) s e l f i t (sit) h a t (sit) i n f i t s (sit) t i s e t s i f e f i g m i s s a t i s (sit) i f t i p

(this) h i t t h e h i m i n (this) i t i s t e e t h i f (this) t h a t p i t d i d (this) i n i s i t f

Part 3
Copy the sentences.

Dad can see the cats sleep.

Dad can see the cats sleep.

Plant this seed in the sand.

Plant this seed in the sand.

Did the lamp seem dim?

Did the lamp seem dim?

That cat sleeps in a tree.

That cat sleeps in a tree.

2

LESSON 3

Name _____

Part 1

Copy the sentences:

If she is sick, I will go to the drug store.

If she is sick, I will go to the drug store.

Last week, we had fun at the track meet.

Last week, we had fun at the track meet.

That truck can go as fast as a deer.

That truck can go as fast as a deer.

Part 2

Read the sentences in the box.

| 1. Last week, we had fun at the track meet. |
| 2. Is that street as slick as it seems? |
| 3. This is the last store we will go to. |

Write the first word of these sentences:

2nd sentence _____ Is

1st sentence _____ Last

3rd sentence _____ This

Part 3

Match the words.

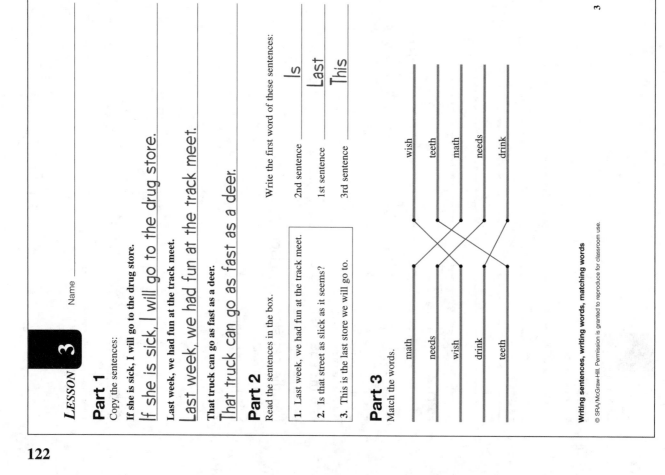

math   wish

needs   teeth

wish   math

drink   needs

teeth   drink

Writing sentences, writing words, matching words

LESSON 4

Name _____

Part 1

ch   d e f a c l p o e (ch) s e a s h m n j s a (ch) e i p l t h n z s l (ch) f d s h f e c r q w x o s

flag   d w (flag) e r o p l e g c z d a (flag) j h e r c l a m c I p e (flag) s a t e f l a t v b s p l a n

Part 2

Copy the sentences:

Will that milk last for a week?

Will that milk last for a week?

I need to keep that pack for the trip.

I need to keep that pack for the trip.

Fill the gas tank in that green truck.

Fill the gas tank in that green truck.

Part 3

Match the words and complete them.

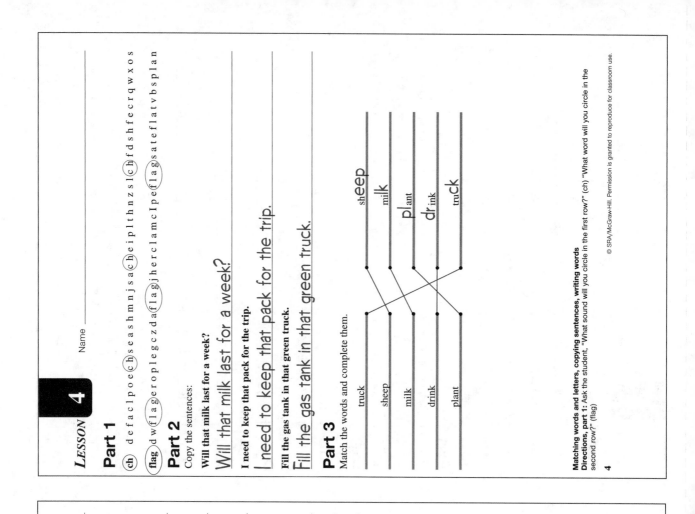

truck   sh_eep_

sheep   mi_lk_

milk   pl_ant_

drink   dr_ink_

plant   tru_ck_

Matching words and letters, copying sentences, writing words
Directions, part 1: Ask the student, "What sound will you circle in the first row?" (ch) "What word will you circle in the second row?" (flag)
4
© SRA/McGraw-Hill. Permission is granted to reproduce for classroom use.

LESSON 5

Name _____

Part 1
Match the words and complete them.

steep   dr_{ink} → dr_{ink}

flag   st_{ore}

drink   fl_{ag}

truck   st_{eep}

store   tr_{uck}

Part 2
Copy the sentences:

We have a plan for a fun trip.

We have a plan for a fun trip.

She sat with Pam at the track meet.

She sat with Pam at the track meet.

His clock did not run.

His clock did not run.

Part 3
Read the sentences in the box.

1. Fill that gold cup with milk.
2. That truck had a flat.
3. She did not sit with us.

Write the first word of these sentences:

3rd sentence _____ She

1st sentence _____ Fill

2nd sentence _____ That

Writing words, copying sentences

5

LESSON 6

Name _____

Part 1
Copy the sentences:

He will go with the man in that truck.

He will go with the man in that truck.

Will Pat feed the cats?

Will Pat feed the cats?

A steep hill had grass on it.

A steep hill had grass on it.

Sand is still in the street.

Sand is still in the street.

Part 2

(on) l i n r s t a n b c s (on) a t h e h l u l (on) e t a c k (on) a e l i n o l s d (on) r a (on) a (on) l e s t q

(for) o n (for) t s (for) l d t o t e (for) o r t a l (for) k f a n e (for) l p k d o (for) t a s f i l l w

(to) s o t (to) d p f o s a w (to) k e t a o w a l t h (to) s h (to) u s h t r c (to) j p i a t (to) e h l i t t (to) a

Part 3
Read the sentences in the box. Write the first word of these sentences.

1. The man told him, "Hop in this truck."
2. "We do not have a clock," Jim said.
3. She said, "Fill this sack with fish."

2nd sentence _____ We

1st sentence _____ The

3rd sentence _____ She

Writing sentences, finding words, writing words

6

124

Part 1

Match the words and complete them.

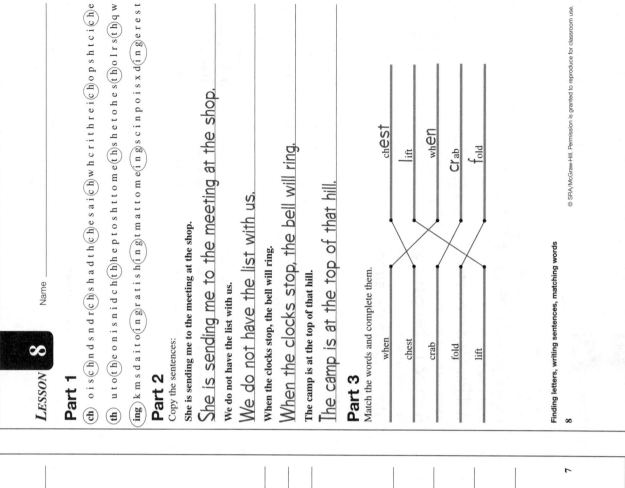

sing   loCks
hill
cheer   chEEr
locks   saCk
sack   sIng
   hIll

Part 2

Read the sentences in the box. Write the first word of these sentences.

1. Drop it in the box.
2. How much cash do you need?
3. That man has an old cat.

1st sentence   Drop
3rd sentence   That
2nd sentence   How

Part 3

Copy the sentences:

When they score, we will cheer.

When they score, we will cheer.

How well did she do in the math class?

How well did she do in the math class?

They sell chips and dip in that shop.

They sell chips and dip in that shop.

Will you sell that horse?

Will you sell that horse?

Writing words, copying sentences

Part 1

ch) ois **ch** ndsndr **ch** shadth **ch** esai **ch** whcrithrei **ch** opshtci **ch** he

th) uto **th** eonisnidch **th** heptoshttome **th** shetohes **th** olrs **th** qw

ing) kmsdaito **ing** ratish **ing** tmattome **ing** scinpoisxd **ing** erest

Part 2

Copy the sentences:

She is sending me to the meeting at the shop.

She is sending me to the meeting at the shop.

We do not have the list with us.

We do not have the list with us.

When the clocks stop, the bell will ring.

When the clocks stop, the bell will ring.

The camp is at the top of that hill.

The camp is at the top of that hill.

Part 3

Match the words and complete them.

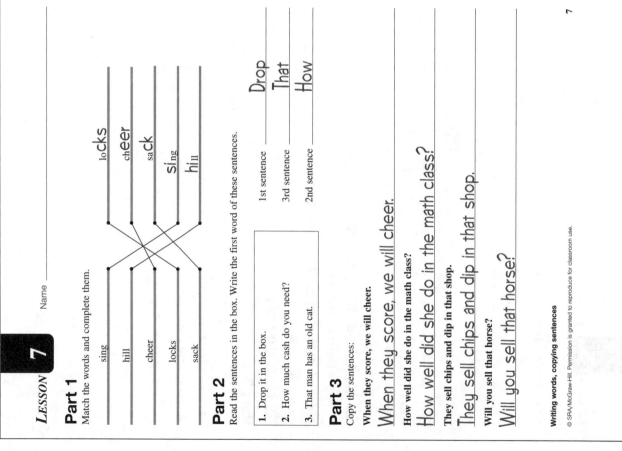

when   chEst
chest   lift
crab   whEn
fold   crab
lift   fold

Finding letters, writing sentences, matching words

LESSON 9

Name _____

Part 1

Read the sentences in the box. Write the first word of these sentences.

1. When will we win a track meet?
2. They were not singing.
3. Can you get that truck to run?

2nd sentence _____ They

3rd sentence _____ Can

1st sentence _____ When

Part 2

Copy the sentences:

The cow went faster than the old truck.

The cow went faster than the old truck.

That man was the last person on the bus.

That man was the last person on the bus.

Bring them back to class in the morning.

Bring them back to class in the morning.

Run to the top of that hill.

Run to the top of that hill.

Part 3

Match the words and complete them.

chops   muCh

crash   chOps

much   shell

clerk   craSh

shell   clerk

Writing words, writing sentences, matching words

9

LESSON 10

Name _____

Part 1

Copy the sentences:

Were you going to bring her letter with you?

Were you going to bring her letter with you?

Jerry and I will have fish and chips for lunch.

Jerry and I will have fish and chips for lunch.

That woman went for a run this morning.

That woman went for a run this morning.

After a nap, he felt much better.

After a nap, he felt much better.

Part 2

Read the sentences in the box. Write the first word of these sentences.

1. Was she with him when you met her?
2. They sell clocks in that store.
3. Bring that glass of milk here.

1st sentence _____ Was

3rd sentence _____ Bring

2nd sentence _____ They

Part 3

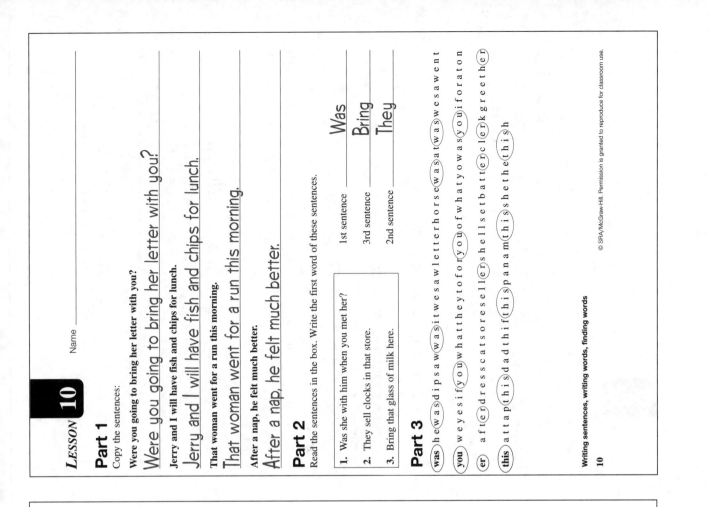

was hewasdipsaw(was)itwesawletterhorse(was)at(was)wesawent

you weyesif(you)whattheytofor(you)ofwhatyowas(you)iforaton

er   af(ter)dresscatsoresell(er)shellsetbatt(er)clerk(er)greet(her)

this attap(this)dadthif(this)panam(this)shethe(this)h

Writing sentences, writing words, finding words

10

125

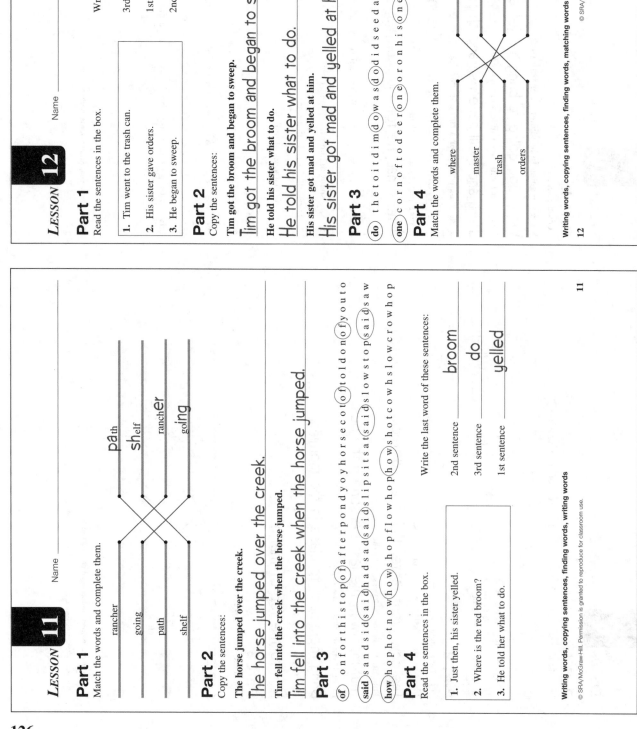

LESSON 12

Name _____

Part 1
Read the sentences in the box.

1. Tim went to the trash can.
2. His sister gave orders.
3. He began to sweep.

Write the last word of these sentences:

3rd sentence ___ sweep

1st sentence ___ can

2nd sentence ___ orders

Part 2
Copy the sentences:

Tim got the broom and began to sweep.
Tim got the broom and began to sweep.

He told his sister what to do.
He told his sister what to do.

His sister got mad and yelled at him.
His sister got mad and yelled at him.

Part 3
do thetoitdim(do)was(do)did seed a(d d)o told sit(do)clip is(do)to

one cornoftodeer(one)oronhis(one)totornit(one)sadonit(one)

Part 4
Match the words and complete them.

where — traSh

master — orderS

trash — mastEr

orders — wHere

Writing words, copying sentences, finding words, matching words

12

LESSON 11

Name _____

Part 1
Match the words and complete them.

rancher — pAth

going — shElf

path —ранchEr

shelf — goIng

Part 2
Copy the sentences:

The horse jumped over the creek.
The horse jumped over the creek.

Tim fell into the creek when the horse jumped.
Tim fell into the creek when the horse jumped.

Part 3
of onforthistop(of)afterpondyoyhorsecot(of)toldon(of)fyouto

said sandsid(said)had sad(said)slipsitsat(said)slowstops(said)saw

how hophotnow(how)shopflowhop(how)shotcowhslowcrowhop

Part 4
Read the sentences in the box.

1. Just then, his sister yelled.
2. Where is the red broom?
3. He told her what to do.

Write the last word of these sentences:

2nd sentence ___ broom

3rd sentence ___ do

1st sentence ___ yelled

Writing words, copying sentences, finding words, writing words

11

126

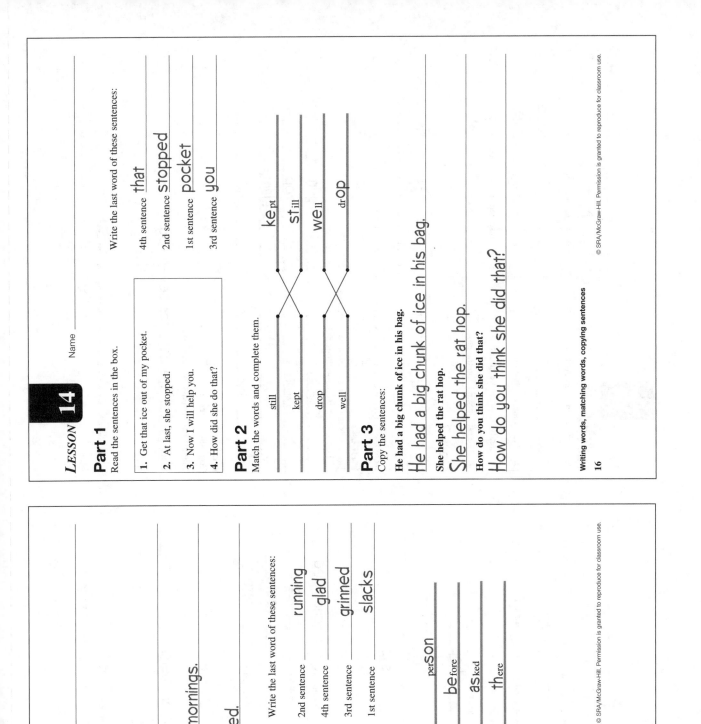

LESSON 13   Name _____

Part 1
Copy the sentences:

She was wearing her slippers.

She was wearing her slippers.

He didn't wear socks on cold mornings.

He didn't wear socks on cold mornings.

His mom told him what happened.

His mom told him what happened.

Part 2
Read the sentences in the box.

1. These socks go with black slacks.
2. He had red socks for running.
3. His little sister grinned.
4. Ron's mom was not glad.

Write the last word of these sentences:

2nd sentence _____ running

4th sentence _____ glad

3rd sentence _____ grinned

1st sentence _____ slacks

Part 3
Match the words and complete them.

there   perSon
asked   before
before   aSked
person   there

Copying sentences, writing words, matching words

14

LESSON 14   Name _____

Part 1
Read the sentences in the box.

1. Get that ice out of my pocket.
2. At last, she stopped.
3. Now I will help you.
4. How did she do that?

Write the last word of these sentences:

4th sentence _____ that

2nd sentence _____ stopped

1st sentence _____ pocket

3rd sentence _____ you

Part 2
Match the words and complete them.

still   kept
kept   still
drop   well
well   drop

Part 3
Copy the sentences:

He had a big chunk of ice in his bag.

He had a big chunk of ice in his bag.

She helped the rat hop.

She helped the rat hop.

How do you think she did that?

How do you think she did that?

Writing words, matching words, copying sentences

16

128

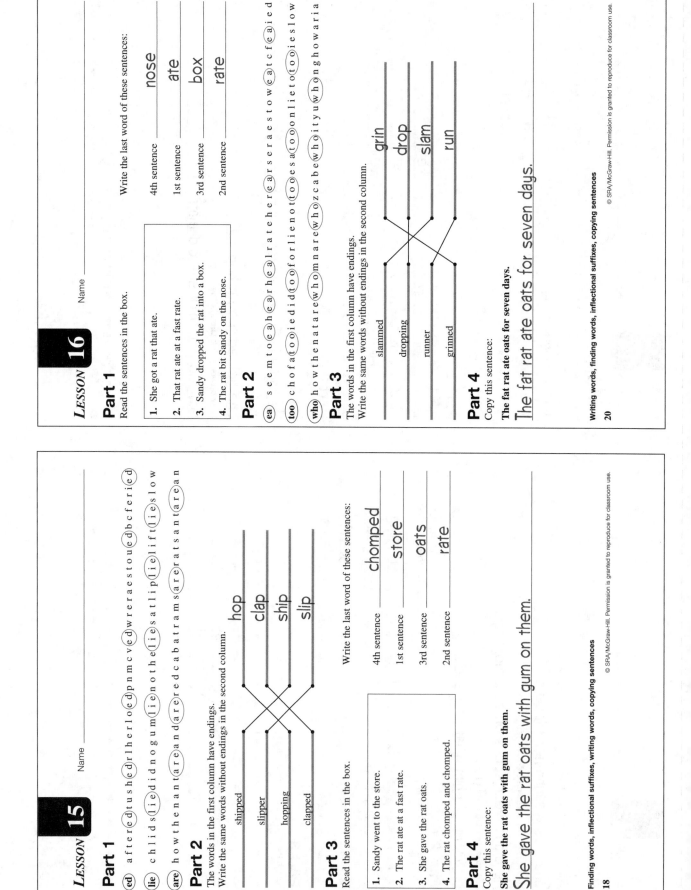

LESSON 15

Name _____

Part 1

ed a f t e r (ed) t u s h (ed) r l h e r l o (ed) p n m c v (ed) w r e r a e s t o u (ed) b c f e r i (ed)

lie c h l i d s (lie) l i d d i d n o g u m (lie) n o t h e (lie) s a t l i p (lie) l i f t (lie) s l o w

are h o w t h e n a n t (are) a n d (are) r e d c a b a t r a m s (are) r a t s a n t (are) a n

Part 2

The words in the first column have endings.
Write the same words without endings in the second column.

shipped — hop
slipper — clap
hopping — ship
clapped — slip

Part 3

Read the sentences in the box.

1. Sandy went to the store.
2. The rat ate at a fast rate.
3. She gave the rat oats.
4. The rat chomped and chomped.

Write the last word of these sentences:

4th sentence   chomped
1st sentence   store
3rd sentence   oats
2nd sentence   rate

Part 4

Copy this sentence:

She gave the rat oats with gum on them.

She gave the rat oats with gum on them.

Finding words, inflectional suffixes, writing words, copying sentences

18

LESSON 16

Name _____

Part 1

Read the sentences in the box.

1. She got a rat that ate.
2. That rat ate at a fast rate.
3. Sandy dropped the rat into a box.
4. The rat bit Sandy on the nose.

Write the last word of these sentences:

4th sentence   nose
1st sentence   ate
3rd sentence   box
2nd sentence   rate

Part 2

ea s e e m t o e (ea) h e a r h (ea) l r a t e h e r e (ea) r s e r a e s t o w (ea) t c f e (ea) i e d

too c h o f a t (too) o i e d i d (too) o f o r l i e n o t (too) e s a (too) o n l i e t o (too) i e s l o w

who h o w t h e n a t a r e (who) m n a r e (who) z c a b e (who) i t y u (who) n g h o w a r i a

Part 3

The words in the first column have endings.
Write the same words without endings in the second column.

slammed — grin
dropping — drop
runner — slam
grimned — run

Part 4

Copy this sentence:

The fat rat ate oats for seven days.

The fat rat ate oats for seven days.

Writing words, finding words, inflectional suffixes, copying sentences

20

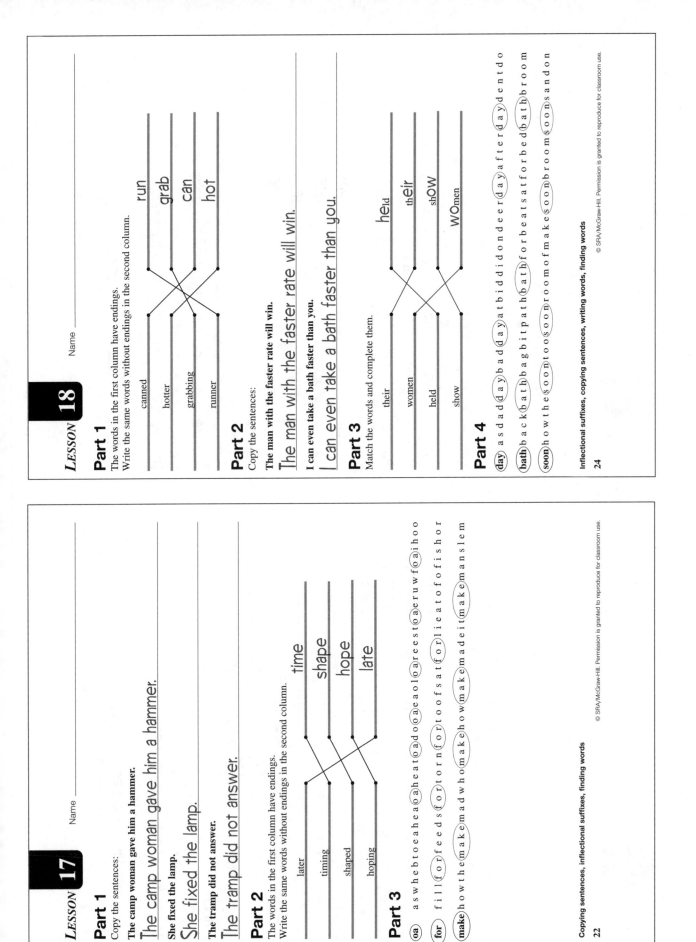

LESSON 17 — Name

Part 1
Copy the sentences:

The camp woman gave him a hammer.

The camp woman gave him a hammer.

She fixed the lamp.

She fixed the lamp.

The tramp did not answer.

The tramp did not answer.

Part 2
The words in the first column have endings.
Write the same words without endings in the second column.

later   time
timing   shape
shaped   hope
hoping   late

Part 3

oa a s w h e b t o e a h e a (oa) h e a t (oa) d o (oa) e a o l (oa) r e e s t (oa) e r u w f (oa) i h o o

for f i l l (for) f e e d s (for) t o r n (for) t o o f s a t (for) l i e a t o f o f i s h o r

make h o w t h e (make) m a d w h o (make) h o w (make) m a d e i t (make) m a n s l e m

Copying sentences, inflectional suffixes, finding words

22

© SRA/McGraw-Hill. Permission is granted to reproduce for classroom use.

LESSON 18 — Name

Part 1
The words in the first column have endings.
Write the same words without endings in the second column.

canned   run
hotter   grab
grabbing   can
runner   hot

Part 2
Copy the sentences:

The man with the faster rate will win.

The man with the faster rate will win.

I can even take a bath faster than you.

I can even take a bath faster than you.

Part 3
Match the words and complete them.

their   he ld
women   th eir
held   sh ow
show   w o men

Part 4

day a s d a d (day) b a d (day) a t b i d d i d d o n d e e r (day) a f t e r (day) d e n t d o

bath b a c k (bath) b a g b i t p a t h (bath) f o r b e a t s a t f o r b e d (bath) b r o o m

soon h o w t h e (soon) t o o (soon) r o o m o f m a k e (soon) b r o o m (soon) s a n d o n

Inflectional suffixes, copying sentences, writing words, finding words

24

© SRA/McGraw-Hill. Permission is granted to reproduce for classroom use.

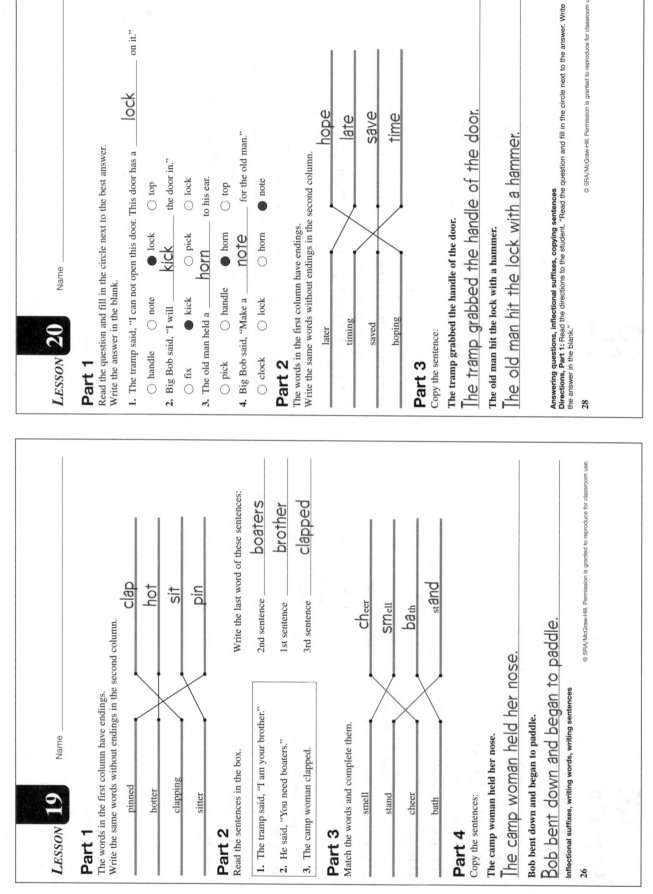

LESSON 19 — Name _____

Part 1

The words in the first column have endings.
Write the same words without endings in the second column.

pinned   clap
hotter   hot
clapping   sit
sitter   pin

Part 2

Read the sentences in the box.

> 1. The tramp said, "I am your brother."
> 2. He said, "You need boaters."
> 3. The camp woman clapped.

Write the last word of these sentences:

2nd sentence ____boaters____
1st sentence ____brother____
3rd sentence ____clapped____

Part 3

Match the words and complete them.

smell   ch**eer**
stand   sm**ell**
cheer   ba**th**
bath   st**and**

Part 4

Copy the sentences:

The camp woman held her nose.

The camp woman held her nose.

Bob bent down and began to paddle.

Bob bent down and began to paddle.

Inflectional suffixes, writing words, writing sentences

26   © SRA/McGraw-Hill. Permission is granted to reproduce for classroom use.

LESSON 20 — Name _____

Part 1

Read the question and fill in the circle next to the best answer.
Write the answer in the blank.

1. The tramp said, "I can not open this door. This door has a ____lock____ on it."
   ○ handle   ○ note   ● lock   ○ top

2. Big Bob said, "I will ____kick____ the door in."
   ○ fix   ● kick   ○ pick   ○ lock

3. The old man held a ____horn____ to his ear.
   ○ pick   ○ handle   ● horn   ○ top

4. Big Bob said, "Make a ____note____ for the old man."
   ○ clock   ○ lock   ○ horn   ● note

Part 2

The words in the first column have endings.
Write the same words without endings in the second column.

later   hope
timing   late
saved   save
hoping   time

Part 3

Copy the sentence:

The tramp grabbed the handle of the door.

The tramp grabbed the handle of the door.

The old man hit the lock with a hammer.

The old man hit the lock with a hammer.

Answering questions, inflectional suffixes, copying sentences
Directions, Part 1: Read the directions to the student. "Read the question and fill in the circle next to the answer. Write the answer in the blank."

28   © SRA/McGraw-Hill. Permission is granted to reproduce for classroom use.

Name _____

Part 1

Read the question and fill in the circle next to the answer.
Write the answer in the blank.

1. The con man had a box of ___mops___ .

   ○ locks   ○ clocks   ● mops   ○ tops

2. The tramp was a fast ___slop___ raker.

   ○ slope   ● slop   ○ shore   ○ shop

3. The tramp said, "I will ___prop___ this mop near the door."

   ● prop   ○ slop   ○ stop   ○ bop

4. The con man sold the camp woman ___bad___ mops.

   ○ seven   ○ thin   ○ 50   ● bad

Part 2

The words in the first column have endings.
Write the same words without endings in the second column.

mopping —————————— mop

grabbed ——————\ /—— drop

dropper ———\ /—X—— slip

slipping ———X—/ \—— grab

Part 3

Copy the sentence:

The con man was glad to sell the mops.

___The con man was glad to sell the mops.___

Answering questions, inflectional suffixes, copying sentences

© SRA/McGraw-Hill. Permission is granted to reproduce for classroom use.

Name _____

Part 1

Match the words and complete them.

matter —————— be_cause_

because ——X—— sha_ck_

lifted ——X—— lif_t_ed

shack —————— mat_ter_

Part 2

Copy the sentences:

Cathy worked in a dress shop.

___Cathy worked in a dress shop.___

Cathy and Pam left the shed and sat on a bench.

___Cathy and Pam left the shed and sat on a bench.___

Part 3

Read the question and fill in the circle next to the answer.
Write the answer in the blank.

1. Pam led Cathy to a ___fish shed___

   ○ dress shop   ○ big camp   ○ clock store   ● fish shed

2. The man in a big coat said, "I am a ___fish packer___ ".

   ○ cook   ○ worker   ● fish packer   ○ slop raker

3. The man had a basket of fish in his ___boat___ .

   ○ shed   ● boat   ○ shop   ○ store

4. The man in the fish shed gave Pam and Cathy ___free___ chips.

   ● free   ○ five   ○ fish   ○ flat

Writing words, copying sentences, answering questions

© SRA/McGraw-Hill. Permission is granted to reproduce for classroom use.

132

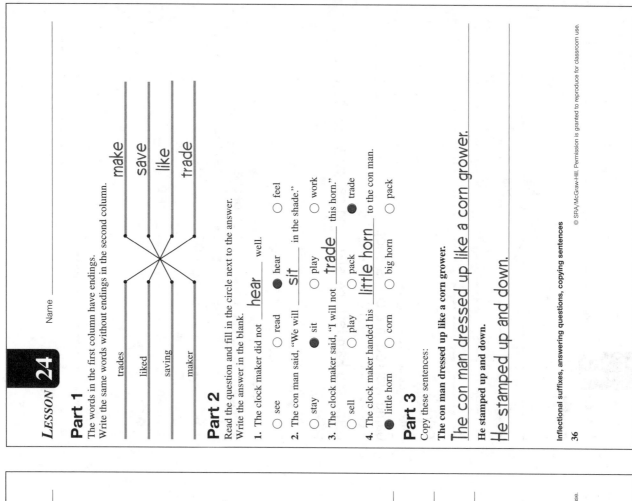

LESSON 24

Name _____

Part 1

The words in the first column have endings.
Write the same words without endings in the second column.

trades	make
liked	save
saving	like
maker	trade

Part 2

Read the question and fill in the circle next to the answer.
Write the answer in the blank.

1. The clock maker did not __hear__ well.
   ○ see ● hear ○ read ○ feel

2. The con man said, "We will __sit__ in the shade."
   ○ stay ● sit ○ play ○ work

3. The clock maker said, "I will not __trade__ this horn."
   ○ sell ○ play ○ pack ● trade

4. The clock maker handed his __little horn__ to the con man.
   ● little horn ○ corn ○ big horn ○ pack

Part 3

Copy these sentences:

The con man dressed up like a corn grower.

The con man dressed up like a corn grower.

He stamped up and down.

He stamped up and down.

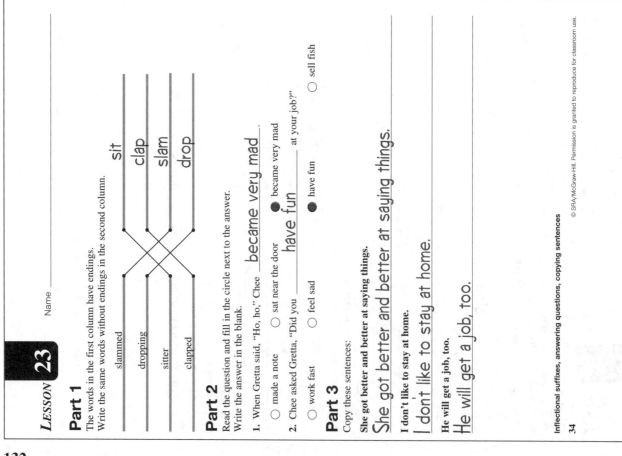

LESSON 23

Name _____

Part 1

The words in the first column have endings.
Write the same words without endings in the second column.

slammed	sit
dropping	clap
sitter	slam
clapped	drop

Part 2

Read the question and fill in the circle next to the answer.
Write the answer in the blank.

1. When Gretta said, "Ho, ho," Chee __became very mad__.
   ○ made a note ○ sat near the door ● became very mad

2. Chee asked Gretta, "Did you __have fun__ at your job?"
   ○ work fast ○ feel sad ● have fun ○ sell fish

Part 3

Copy these sentences:

She got better and better at saying things.

She got better and better at saying things.

I don't like to stay at home.

I don't like to stay at home.

He will get a job, too.

He will get a job, too.

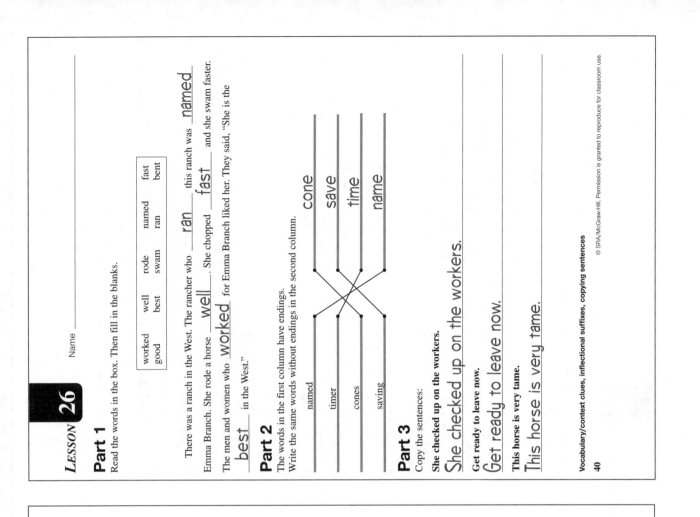

LESSON 26 Name _____

Part 1
Read the words in the box. Then fill in the blanks.

| worked | well | rode | named | fast |
| good | best | swam | ran | bent |

There was a ranch in the West. The rancher who __ran__ this ranch was __named__ Emma Branch. She rode a horse __well__. She chopped __fast__ and she swam faster.

The men and women who __worked__ for Emma Branch liked her. They said, "She is the __best__ in the West."

Part 2
The words in the first column have endings.
Write the same words without endings in the second column.

named — cone
timer — save
cones — time
saving — name

Part 3
Copy the sentences:

She checked up on the workers.
She checked up on the workers.

Get ready to leave now.
Get ready to leave now.

This horse is very tame.
This horse is very tame.

Vocabulary/context clues, inflectional suffixes, copying sentences
40   © SRA/McGraw-Hill. Permission is granted to reproduce for classroom use.

LESSON 25 Name _____

Part 1
Match the words and complete them.

felt — le_ft_
help — se_lf_
left — fe_lt_
self — hel_p_

Part 2
Copy the sentences:

Chee began to say odd things.
Chee began to say odd things.

She left her home to get a job.
She left her home to get a job.

He had tears on his cheeks.
He had tears on his cheeks.

The man came back with his boss.
The man came back with his boss.

Part 3
The words in the first column have endings.
Write the same words without endings in the second column.

getting — big
dropper — get
grabbed — drop
bigger — grab

Writing words, copying sentences, inflectional suffixes
38   © SRA/McGraw-Hill. Permission is granted to reproduce for classroom use.

LESSON 27

Name _____

Part 1
Read the words in the box. Then fill in the blanks.

fastest	packer	stick	plant	old
stackers	slowest	odd	mad	slate
pack	made	slat	job	stack

Chee got a **job** at a **slate** plant. When she was not **mad**, she did not say **odd** things. The woman who ran the **plant** showed Chee how to **stack** slate. At the end of one year, Chee was one of the fastest **stackers**.

Part 2
Copy the sentences:

The woman showed Chee how to stack slate.
The woman showed Chee how to stack slate.

She worked at the plant for nearly a year.
She worked at the plant for nearly a year.

Set that slab on top of the pile.
Set that slab on top of the pile.

Part 3
The words in the first column have endings.
Write the same words without endings in the second column.

clapped — big
running — swim
swimmer — run
biggest — clap

Vocabulary/context clues, copying sentences, inflectional suffixes

42

© SRA/McGraw-Hill. Permission is granted to reproduce for classroom use.

LESSON 28

Name _____

Part 1
Read the words in the box. Then fill in the blanks.

leave	shop	sheep	sacks	best
steal	work	shave	plan	faster
packs	shears	wool	well	fake

The con man said, "I can **shave** a sheep before it sees the **shears**. You can **shop**, but you cannot get someone who can shave **faster** than me."

The con man told the rancher to get him ten **sacks** for holding the **wool**. He did not plan to shear **sheep**. He planned to **steal** them.

Part 2
Match the words and complete them.

before — chest
steal — still
still — steal
chest — before

Part 3
Copy the sentences:

He got the shears from his pack.
He got the shears from his pack.

He planned to pack sheep into sacks.
He planned to pack sheep into sacks.

The rancher sat on the con man and shaved his locks.
The rancher sat on the con man and shaved his locks.

Vocabulary/context clues, writing words, copying sentences

44

© SRA/McGraw-Hill. Permission is granted to reproduce for classroom use.

LESSON 29

Name _____

Part 1

Read the words in the box. Then fill in the blanks.

tamps	ranch	rest	pack	old
odd	slop	camp	say	stay
sack	ramps	hill	lake	leave

The tramp worked at the __camp__ for nearly a year. He tamped and made __ramps__.

Now he said, "I will __leave__ this camp. Tramps don't __stay__ in a camp for more

than a year."

So the tramp got his __pack__. He told the camp woman, "The work here is getting

__old__, and I need a __rest__."

Part 2

The words in the first column have endings.
Write the same words without endings in the second column.

maker ———— ride
ropes ———— make
shaved ———— rope
riding ———— shave

Part 3

Copy the sentences:

He worked there for nearly a year.

He worked there for nearly a year.

When the sun comes up, he will shear sheep.

When the sun comes up, he will shear sheep.

Vocabulary/context clues, inflectional suffixes, copying sentences

46

© SRA/McGraw-Hill. Permission is granted to reproduce for classroom use.

LESSON 30

Name _____

Part 1

Read the question and fill in the circle next to the answer.
Write the answer in the blank.

1. The tramp was sleeping near a sheep __shed__.
   ○ camp   ● shed   ○ shop   ○ ranch

2. The tramp felt more like __sleeping__ than shearing.
   ○ sweeping   ○ shaving   ○ yelling   ● sleeping

3. Emma said, "You have __50__ minutes to shear __50__ sheep."
   ○ five   ● 50   ○ 20   ○ ten

4. Emma kept her __deal__ with the tramp.
   ○ plan   ○ ranch   ● deal   ○ hand

Part 2

Copy the sentences:

The sun came up in the morning.

The sun came up in the morning.

The cook will make a good meal.

The cook will make a good meal.

Part 3

The words in the first column have endings.
Write the same words without endings in the second column.

sweeping ———— help
reached ———— reach
helper ———— sweep

Answering questions, copying sentences, inflectional suffixes

48

© SRA/McGraw-Hill. Permission is granted to reproduce for classroom use.

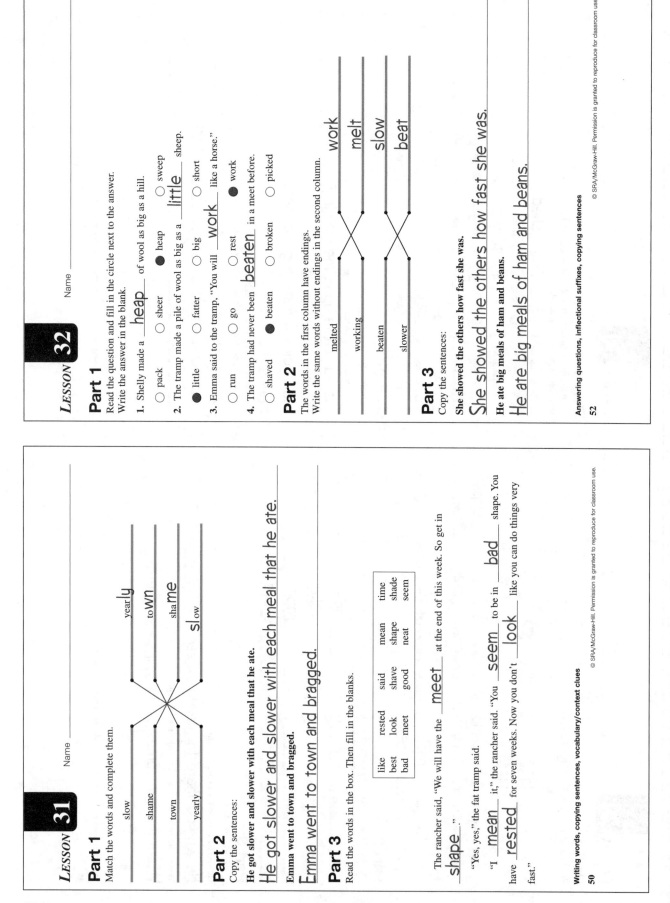

LESSON 32 — Name _____

Part 1

Read the question and fill in the circle next to the answer. Write the answer in the blank.

1. Shelly made a __heap__ of wool as big as a hill.
   ○ pack ○ sheer ● heap ○ sweep

2. The tramp made a pile of wool as big as a __little__ sheep.
   ● little ○ fatter ○ big ○ short

3. Emma said to the tramp, "You will __work__ like a horse."
   ○ run ○ go ○ rest ● work

4. The tramp had never been __beaten__ in a meet before.
   ○ shaved ● beaten ○ broken ○ picked

Part 2

The words in the first column have endings. Write the same words without endings in the second column.

melted — work
working — melt
beaten — slow
slower — beat

Part 3

Copy the sentences:

She showed the others how fast she was.

She showed the others how fast she was.

He ate big meals of ham and beans.

He ate big meals of ham and beans.

Answering questions, inflectional suffixes, copying sentences

52

LESSON 31 — Name _____

Part 1

Match the words and complete them.

slow — yearly
shame — town
town — shame
yearly — slow

Part 2

Copy the sentences:

He got slower and slower with each meal that he ate.

He got slower and slower with each meal that he ate.

Emma went to town and bragged.

Emma went to town and bragged.

Part 3

Read the words in the box. Then fill in the blanks.

like	rested	said	mean	time
best	look	shave	shape	shade
bad	meet	good	neat	seem

The rancher said, "We will have the __meet__ at the end of this week. So get in __shape__."

"Yes, yes," the fat tramp said.

"I __mean__ it," the rancher said. "You __seem__ to be in __bad__ shape. You have __rested__ for seven weeks. Now you don't __look__ like you can do things very fast."

Writing words, copying sentences, vocabulary/context clues

50

136

LESSON 33   Name _____

Part 1

The words in the first column have endings.
Write the same words without endings in the second column.

beginning ——— plant
planter ——— begin
peeking ——— work
worked ——— peek

Part 2

Read the words in the box. Then fill in the blanks.

shaping	shaving	faster	week	work
fatter	sore	sheared	hot	meals
cold	hands	hammer	made	shape

The rancher gave the tramp more work. At the end of the day, the tramp was __sore__.

But at the end of the week, he began to get __faster__. His __hammer__ began to go like a flash. His shears began to get __hot__ when he was __shaving__ sheep. The tramp was beginning to get back in __shape__.

Part 3

Copy the sentences:

His hammer began to go like a flash.

His hammer began to go like a flash.

There was no more work at the ranch.

There was no more work at the ranch.

Inflectional suffixes, vocabulary/context clues, copying sentences

---

LESSON 34   Name _____

Part 1

Read the question and fill in the circle next to the answer.
Write the answer in the blank.

1. Shelly said, "I have never been __beaten__ in a shearing meet."

   ○ broken   ○ cheered   ● beaten   ○ shaved

2. At the end of the meet, the tramp had sheared __9000__ sheep.

   ○ 5000   ● 9000   ○ 210   ○ 501

3. Shelly had sheared __501__ sheep.

   ○ 5000   ○ 9000   ○ 210   ● 501

Part 2

The words in the first column have endings.
Write the same words without endings in the second column.

cheered ——— pant
panting ——— ranch
beaten ——— cheer
rancher ——— beat

Part 3

Copy the sentences:

She is the best worker at the plant.

She is the best worker at the plant.

The people from town waved to the tramp.

The people from town waved to the tramp.

Her helpers began to bag the wool.

Her helpers began to bag the wool.

Answering questions, inflectional suffixes, copying sentences

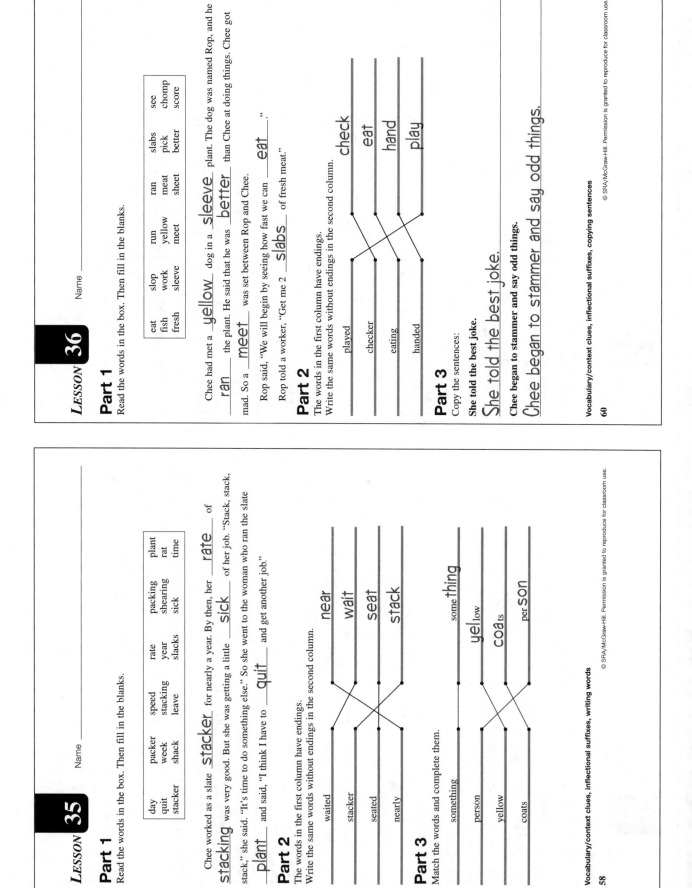

138

LESSON 35   Name _____

Part 1
Read the words in the box. Then fill in the blanks.

day	packer	speed	rate	packing	plant
quit	week	stacking	year	shearing	rat
stacker	shack	leave	slacks	sick	time

Chee worked as a slate stacker for nearly a year. By then, her rate of stacking was very good. But she was getting a little sick of her job. "Stack, stack, stack," she said. "It's time to do something else." So she went to the woman who ran the slate plant and said, "I think I have to quit and get another job."

Part 2
The words in the first column have endings.
Write the same words without endings in the second column.

waited   near
stacker   wait
seated   seat
nearly   stack

Part 3
Match the words and complete them.

something   some thing
person   yel low
yellow   coa ts
coats   per son

LESSON 36   Name _____

Part 1
Read the words in the box. Then fill in the blanks.

eat	slop	run	ran	slabs	see
fish	work	yellow	meat	pick	chomp
fresh	sleeve	meet	sheet	better	score

Chee had met a yellow dog in a sleeve plant. The dog was named Rop, and he ran the plant. He said that he was better than Chee at doing things. Chee got mad. So a meet was set between Rop and Chee.

Rop said, "We will begin by seeing how fast we can eat."

Rop told a worker, "Get me 2 slabs of fresh meat."

Part 2
The words in the first column have endings.
Write the same words without endings in the second column.

played   check
checker   eat
eating   hand
handed   play

Part 3
Copy the sentences:

She told the best joke.
She told the best joke.

Chee began to stammer and say odd things.
Chee began to stammer and say odd things.

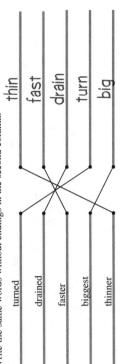
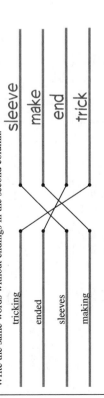

LESSON 38   Name

Part 1
The words in the first column have endings.
Write the same words without endings in the second column.

turned — thin
drained — fast
faster — drain
biggest — turn
thinner — big

Part 2
Write the words.

can + not = cannot
any + body = anybody
my + self = myself
some + one = someone

Part 3
Copy the sentences:

He sold gas at the boat ramp.
He sold gas at the boat ramp.

She did not hear waves on the shore.
She did not hear waves on the shore.

LESSON 37   Name

Part 1
Cross out the words that don't have ea.

rat   mean   hear   main   each   sleep
shear   began   these   tail   smell   beat
seating   real   pail   neck   between   reach

Part 2
Read the words in the box. Then fill in the blanks.

tricking   slapped   lap   sleeves   handed
stammer   making   slabs   slap   store
stabbed   coats   fast   score   wool

Chee and Rop went into the sleeve- making room of the plant. There Rop said, "I will get the best score for this meet. We will see how fast that lap dog can slap sleeves in coats . The dog that slaps sleeves fastest will win." Rop handed Chee a needle, but she stabbed herself with the needle.

Part 3
The words in the first column have endings.
Write the same words without endings in the second column.

tricking — sleeve
ended — make
sleeves — end
making — trick

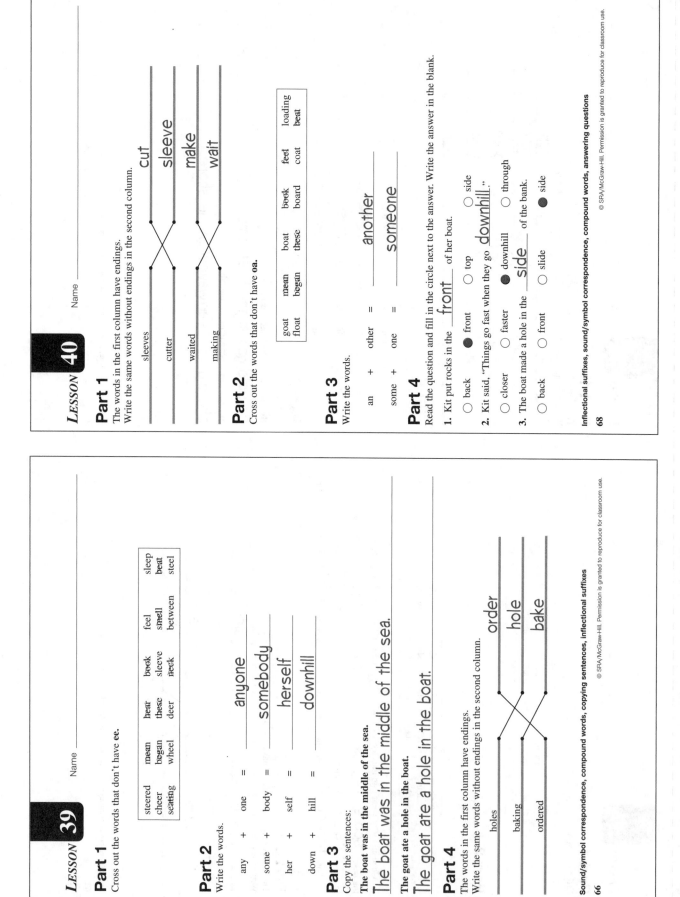

140

LESSON 40

Name _____

Part 1

The words in the first column have endings.
Write the same words without endings in the second column.

sleeves   cut

cutter   sleeve

waited   make

making   wait

Part 2

Cross out the words that don't have **oa**.

goat	mean	boat	book	feet	loading
float	began	these	board	coat	beat

Part 3

Write the words.

an + other = __another__

some + one = __someone__

Part 4

Read the question and fill in the circle next to the answer. Write the answer in the blank.

1. Kit put rocks in the __front__ of her boat.
   ○ back   ● front   ○ top   ○ side

2. Kit said, "Things go fast when they go __downhill__."
   ○ closer   ○ faster   ● downhill   ○ through

3. The boat made a hole in the __side__ of the bank.
   ○ back   ○ front   ○ slide   ● side

Inflectional suffixes, sound/symbol correspondence, compound words, answering questions

68

LESSON 39

Name _____

Part 1

Cross out the words that don't have **ee.**

steered	mean	hear	book	feel	sleep
cheer	began	these	sleeve	smell	beat
seating	wheel	deer	neck	between	steel

Part 2

Write the words.

any + one = __anyone__

some + body = __somebody__

her + self = __herself__

down + hill = __downhill__

Part 3

Copy the sentences:

The boat was in the middle of the sea.

The boat was in the middle of the sea.

The goat ate a hole in the boat.

The goat ate a hole in the boat.

Part 4

The words in the first column have endings.
Write the same words without endings in the second column.

holes   order

baking   hole

ordered   bake

Sound/symbol correspondence, compound words, copying sentences, inflectional suffixes

66

LESSON 41

Name _____

Part 1
Write the words.

good + bye = goodbye

no + thing = nothing

any + body = anybody

down + hill = downhill

six + teen = sixteen

Part 2
Read the words in the box. Then fill in the blanks.

sail	boat	nobody	light	aim	white
bike	save	yellow	nothing	green	slow
red	sell	send	streak	pain	float

Kit said, "I am going to __sell__ this boat and get a __bike__. This boat is

__nothing__ but a __pain__."

Then she said to herself, "I can have a lot of fun with a bike. If I get a __white__ bike, it

will be very __light__, so I'll fly over town."

Part 3
Cross out the words that don't have **ol**.

~~goat~~	told	~~boat~~	~~book~~	fold	~~loading~~
~~float~~	~~began~~	old	cold	~~meal~~	bolted

Compound words, vocabulary/context clues, sound/symbol correspondence

70

LESSON 42

Name _____

Part 1
Cross out the words that don't have **sh**.

shape	~~with~~	~~chest~~	shift	~~what~~
~~which~~	~~chop~~	fish	~~reach~~	~~cheer~~

Part 2
The words in the first column have endings.
Write the same words without endings in the second column.

boating ———— take

opened ———— stroke

stroked ———— boat

taken ———— open

Part 3
Write the words.

every + thing = __everything__

through + out = __throughout__

good + bye = __goodbye__

with + out = __without__

Part 4
Copy the sentences:

The shop man looked at the motor.

The shop man looked at the motor.

She handed three books to him.

She handed three books to him.

Sound/symbol correspondence, inflectional suffixes, compound words, copying sentences

72

141

142

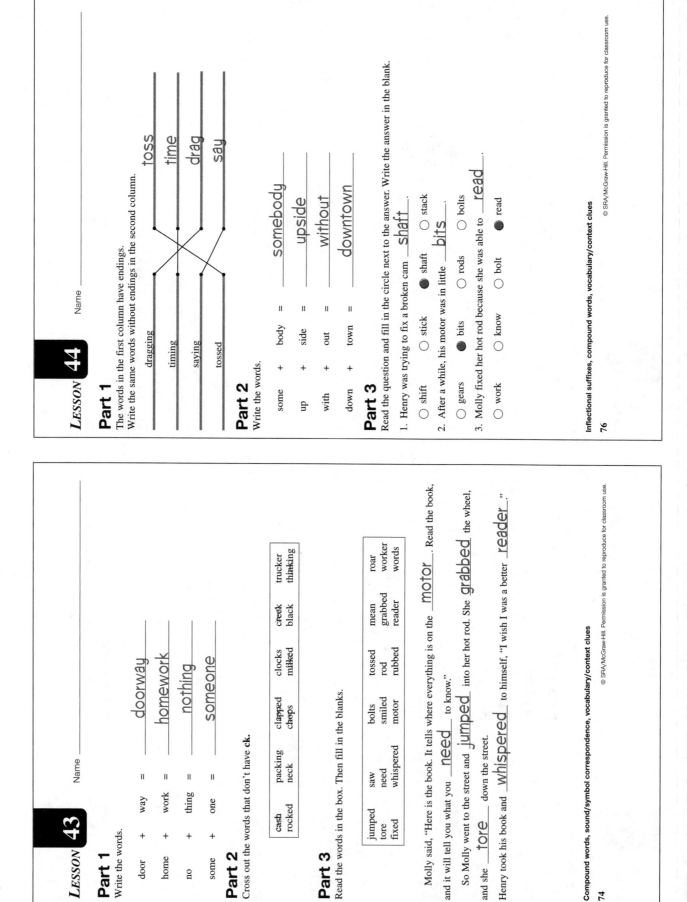

LESSON 43 — Name _____

Part 1
Write the words.

door + way = __doorway__
home + work = __homework__
no + thing = __nothing__
some + one = __someone__

Part 2
Cross out the words that don't have ck.

~~cash~~	packing	~~clapped~~	clocks	~~creek~~	trucker
rocked	neck	~~chops~~	~~milked~~	black	thinking

Part 3
Read the words in the box. Then fill in the blanks.

jumped	saw	bolts	tossed	mean	roar
tore	need	smiled	rod	grabbed	worker
fixed	whispered	motor	rubbed	reader	words

Molly said, "Here is the book. It tells where everything is on the __motor__. Read the book, and it will tell you what you __need__ to know."

So Molly went to the street and __jumped__ into her hot rod. She __grabbed__ the wheel, and she __tore__ down the street.

Henry took his book and __whispered__ to himself, "I wish I was a better __reader__."

Compound words, sound/symbol correspondence, vocabulary/context clues

---

LESSON 44 — Name _____

Part 1
The words in the first column have endings.
Write the same words without endings in the second column.

dragging ———— __toss__
timing ———— __time__
saying ———— __drag__
tossed ———— __say__

Part 2
Write the words.

some + body = __somebody__
up + side = __upside__
with + out = __without__
down + town = __downtown__

Part 3
Read the question and fill in the circle next to the answer. Write the answer in the blank.

1. Henry was trying to fix a broken cam __shaft__.
   ○ shift   ○ stick   ● shaft   ○ stack

2. After a while, his motor was in little __bits__.
   ○ gears   ● bits   ○ rods   ○ bolts

3. Molly fixed her hot rod because she was able to __read__.
   ○ work   ○ know   ○ bolt   ● read

Inflectional suffixes, compound words, vocabulary/context clues

Part 1

Read the words in the box. Then fill in the blanks.

faster	really	lifted	ready	sold	worker
tires	fastest	robber	diver	zip	float
bikes	traded	back	pile	nose	slower

The con man had __traded__ his clock, his cash, his ring, and five __tires__ with holes in them for Kit's tin boat.

Now the con man was __ready__ to become the best bank __robber__ in the west. He said, "I will __pile__ rocks in the __nose__ of this boat. The more rocks I pile, the __faster__ it will go."

Part 2

Match the words and complete them.

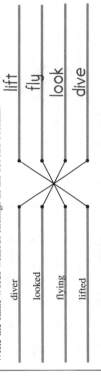

covered — rock__et__

rocket — __idea__

zipped — __co__vered

idea — __zip__ped

Part 3

The words in the first column have endings.
Write the same words without endings in the second column.

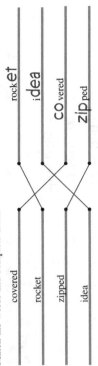

diver — __lift__

looked — __fly__

flying — __look__

lifted — __dive__

Part 1

Write the words.

some	+	body	=	__somebody__	
up	+	set	=	__upset__	
with	+	out	=	__without__	
door	+	way	=	__doorway__	

Part 2

The words in the first column have endings.
Write the same words without endings in the second column.

trenches — __real__

fishing — __trade__

really — __trench__

traded — __fish__

Part 3

Read the words in the box. Then fill in the blanks.

rested	tires	sell	ripped	site	grip
crime	bikes	rid	roads	gripe	deal
conned	steal	ships	ready	paths	robbed

Kit said, "I think I will get __rid__ of this boat. It makes __ships__ sink. It has __ripped__ up 2 docks. It has made __paths__ and trenches. It tore holes in the bank, and that is a bad __crime__."

Kit had a lot to __gripe__ over. So she said, "I will __sell__ the boat."

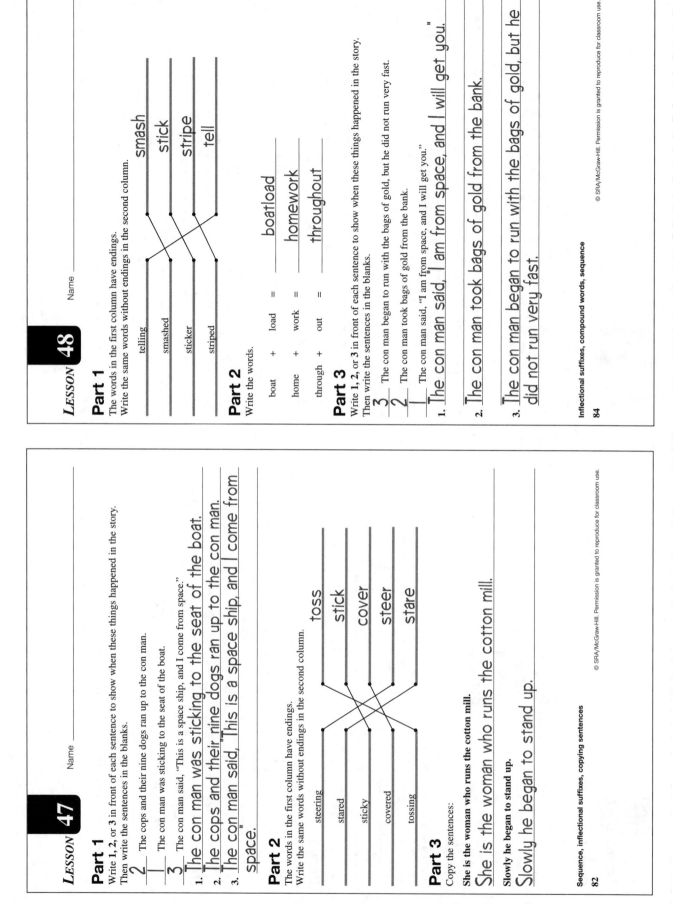

LESSON 47

Name _____

Part 1

Write **1**, **2**, or **3** in front of each sentence to show when these things happened in the story.
Then write the sentences in the blanks.

2 ___ The cops and their nine dogs ran up to the con man.

1 ___ The con man was sticking to the seat of the boat.

3 ___ The con man said, "This is a space ship, and I come from space."

1. The con man was sticking to the seat of the boat.

2. The cops and their nine dogs ran up to the con man.

3. The con man said, "This is a space ship, and I come from space."

Part 2

The words in the first column have endings.
Write the same words without endings in the second column.

steering ——— toss
stared ——— stick
sticky ——— cover
covered ——— steer
tossing ——— stare

Part 3

Copy the sentences:

She is the woman who runs the cotton mill.

She is the woman who runs the cotton mill.

Slowly he began to stand up.

Slowly he began to stand up.

Sequence, inflectional suffixes, copying sentences

LESSON 48

Name _____

Part 1

The words in the first column have endings.
Write the same words without endings in the second column.

telling ——— smash
smashed ——— stick
sticker ——— stripe
striped ——— tell

Part 2

Write the words.

boat + load = boatload

home + work = homework

through + out = throughout

Part 3

Write **1**, **2**, or **3** in front of each sentence to show when these things happened in the story.
Then write the sentences in the blanks.

3 ___ The con man began to run with the bags of gold, but he did not run very fast.

2 ___ The con man took bags of gold from the bank.

1 ___ The con man said, "I am from space, and I will get you."

1. The con man said, "I am from space, and I will get you."

2. The con man took bags of gold from the bank.

3. The con man began to run with the bags of gold, but he did not run very fast.

Inflectional suffixes, compound words, sequence

LESSON 49 — Name

Part 1

Write the word **trying**. Make a line over **ing**. trying

Write the word **moaned.** Make a line under **ed.** moaned

Part 2

The words in the first column have endings.
Write the same words without endings in the second column.

raining   smile
tired   jail
smiling   rain
jailer   tire

Part 3

Read the words in the box. Then fill in the blanks.

yelling	three	grain	seven	hair	pike
five	hard	slipped	rain	thing	leg
slapped	griping	drained	steps	trying	nose
raining	tired	light	jumped	drain	like

It was raining and the con man was griping about the rain. He said,
"My plan is going down the drain." He was trying to run with three bags of gold, but they were not light. He did
not run fast. The cotton in his hair was running down his nose. He did not see
where he was going. He slipped in a pile of slippery pike and fell down.

Part 4

Copy the sentence:

They began to lick the taffy.

They began to lick the taffy.

Sound/symbol correspondence, inflectional suffixes, vocabulary/context clues, copying sentences

86

LESSON 50 — Name

Part 1

Write the word **digging**. Make a line over **ing.** digging

Write the word **lower**. Make a line under **er.** lower

Part 2

Write **1, 2,** or **3** in front of each sentence to show when these things happened in the story.
Then write the sentences in the blanks.

3 The other bugs gave the dusty bug a dime to stay in the cool mine.

1 The bugs went inside a big hole to be in a cool spot.

2 The mother bug saw the dusty bug digging.

1. The bugs went inside a big hole to be in a cool spot.

2. The mother bug saw the dusty bug digging.

3. The other bugs gave the dusty bug a dime to stay in the cool mine.

Part 3

The words in the first column have endings.
Write the same words without endings in the second column.

leaves   hot
lower   walk
hotter   leave
walked   low

Sound/symbol correspondence, sequence, inflectional suffixes

88

145

LESSON 51

Name _____

Part 1
Read the question and fill in the circle next to the answer. Write the answer in the blank.

1. The dusty bug liked ___dills___.
   ○ bills ○ shovels ● dills ○ smells

2. The bug said, "I don't have ___cash___ with me."
   ○ pickles ● cash ○ tubs ○ mine

3. The bug dug into the ___tub___ and got a big pickle.
   ○ store ○ bag ○ mine ● tub

Part 2
Write the word **outside**. Make a line over **out**. ___outside___

Write the word **another**. Make a line under **er**. ___another___

Part 3
Match the words and complete them.

joking — grinned
rotten — cl erk
clerk — jo king
grinned — rot ten

Part 4
Copy this sentence.

The dusty bug smiled from the door of the store.

The dusty bug smiled from the door of the store.

Vocabulary/context clues, sound/symbol correspondence, inflectional suffixes, copying sentences

---

LESSON 52

Name _____

Part 1
Match the words and complete them.

orange — wo man
holding — hold ing
drink — or ange
woman — dr ink

Part 2
Read the words in the box. Then fill in the blanks.

table	grabbed	stopped	bib	fixed	binging
taken	broken	dropped	cheer	deer	door
dropping	floor	fixing	making	sound	leak

The clock maker ___grabbed___ the clock and ___dropped___ it. The clock made a loud ___sound___ when it hit the ___floor___. The ___deer___ fell out. A spring went, "bop."

The clock went, "bing, bing, ding."

The clock maker said, "That clock is ___broken___. Let me make a bid on ___fixing___ it."

Part 3
Write the words.

ding + ing = dinging
real + ly = really
sleep + ing = sleeping
loud + ly = loudly

Writing words, vocabulary/context clues, inflectional/derivational suffixes

LESSON 53 — Name

Part 1
Write **1**, **2**, or **3** in front of each sentence to show when these things happened in the story. Then write the sentences in the blanks.

2. The clock maker slapped a bell into the deer clock.
1. The clock maker painted the deer yellow.
3. The woman tossed the clock down, and it broke into parts.

1. The clock maker painted the deer yellow.
2. The clock maker slapped a bell into the deer clock.
3. The woman tossed the clock down, and it broke into parts.

Part 2
The words in the first column have endings.
Write the same words without endings in the second column.

slapped	work
looked	look
working	part
parts	slap

Part 3
Write the word **himself**. Make a line over **self**.   himself

Write the word **dabbed**. Make a line under **ed**.   dabbed

Part 4
Copy this sentence.

A woman was standing near the door.

A woman was standing near the door.

LESSON 54 — Name

Part 1
Write the words.

every	+	thing	=	everything
with	+	out	=	without
door	+	way	=	doorway
out	+	side	=	outside

Part 2
Write **1**, **2**, or **3** in front of each sentence to show when these things happened in the story. Then write the sentences in the blanks.

3. The old clock maker took the clock back to the woman.
1. An alligator ran across the front of the clock and bit the clock maker's finger.
2. The clock maker stuck antlers on the alligator and slapped it into the deer clock.

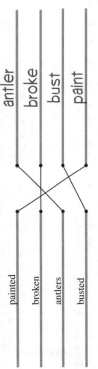

1. An alligator ran across the front of the clock and bit the clock maker's finger.
2. The clock maker stuck antlers on the alligator and slapped it into the deer clock.
3. The old clock maker took the clock back to the woman.

Part 3
The words in the first column have endings.
Write the same words without endings in the second column.

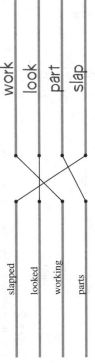

painted	antler
broken	broke
antlers	bust
busted	paint

148

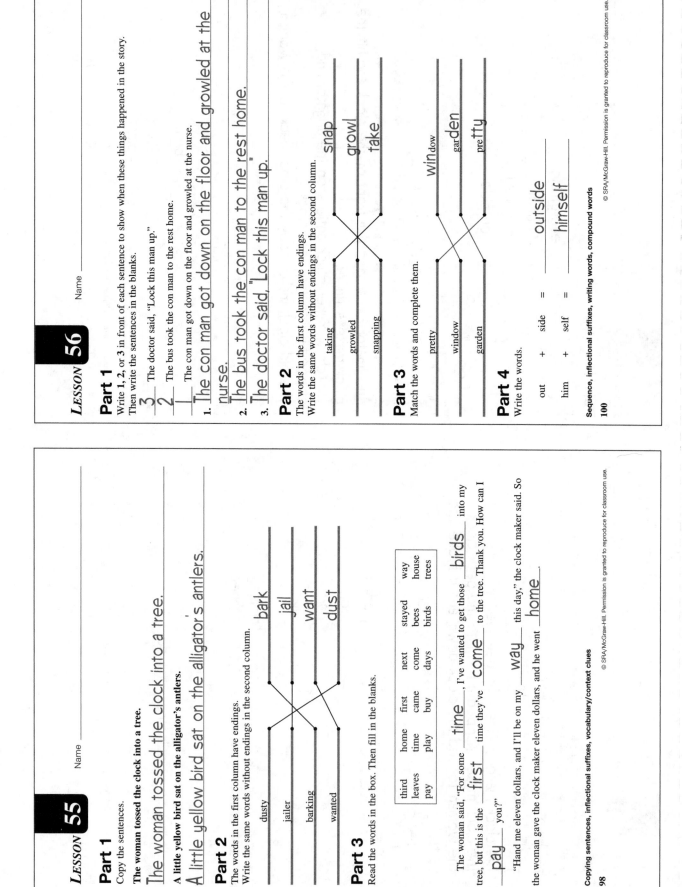

Part 1

Copy the sentences.

The woman tossed the clock into a tree.

The woman tossed the clock into a tree.

A little yellow bird sat on the alligator's antlers.

A little yellow bird sat on the alligator's antlers.

Part 2

The words in the first column have endings.
Write the same words without endings in the second column.

dusty   bark

jailer   jail

barking   want

wanted   dust

Part 3

Read the words in the box. Then fill in the blanks.

third	home	first	next	stayed	way
leaves	time	came	come	bees	house
pay	play	buy	days	birds	trees

The woman said, "For some ___time___, I've wanted to get those ___birds___ into my

tree, but this is the ___first___ time they've ___come___ to the tree. Thank you. How can I

___pay___ you?"

"Hand me eleven dollars, and I'll be on my ___way___ this day," the clock maker said. So

the woman gave the clock maker eleven dollars, and he went ___home___ .

Copying sentences, inflectional suffixes, vocabulary/context clues

98

Part 1

Write **1, 2,** or **3** in front of each sentence to show when these things happened in the story.
Then write the sentences in the blanks.

3 The doctor said, "Lock this man up."

2 The bus took the con man to the rest home.

1 The con man got down on the floor and growled at the nurse.

1. The con man got down on the floor and growled at the nurse.

2. The bus took the con man to the rest home.

3. The doctor said, "Lock this man up."

Part 2

The words in the first column have endings.
Write the same words without endings in the second column.

taking   snap

growled   growl

snapping   take

Part 3

Match the words and complete them.

pretty   win dow

window   garden

garden   pretty

Part 4

Write the words.

out + side = outside

him + self = himself

Sequence, inflectional suffixes, writing words, compound words

100

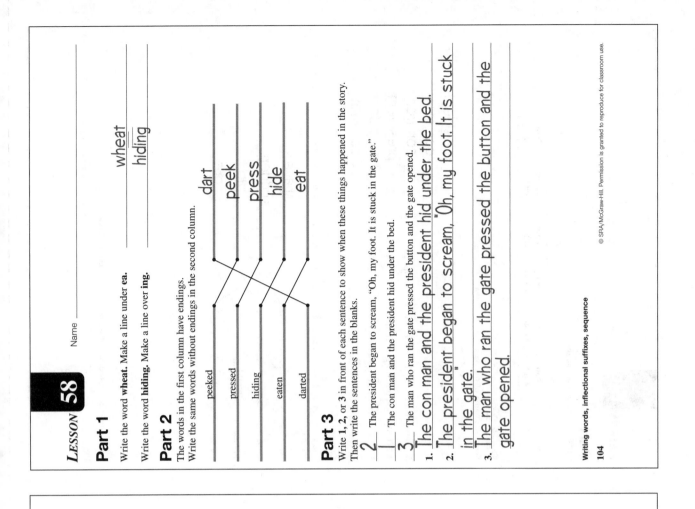

Part 1

Write the word **wheat**. Make a line under **ea**.

wheat

Write the word **hiding**. Make a line over **ing**.

hiding

Part 2

The words in the first column have endings.
Write the same words without endings in the second column.

peeked — dart
pressed — peek
hiding — press
eaten — hide
darted — eat

Part 3

Write **1**, **2**, or **3** in front of each sentence to show when these things happened in the story.
Then write the sentences in the blanks.

2 The president began to scream, "Oh, my foot. It is stuck in the gate."

1 The con man and the president hid under the bed.

3 The man who ran the gate pressed the button and the gate opened.

1. The con man and the president hid under the bed.
2. The president began to scream, "Oh, my foot. It is stuck in the gate."
3. The man who ran the gate pressed the button and the gate opened.

Writing words, inflectional suffixes, sequence

Part 1

Write the words.

be + fore = before
some + where = somewhere
any + one = anyone
your + self = yourself

Part 2

Copy the sentences.

He tried to get out the window.
He tried to get out the window.

They looked around and didn't see anybody.
They looked around and didn't see anybody.

The doctor took notes on a pad.
The doctor took notes on a pad.

Part 3

Write the name of the person each sentence tells about.

president   con man

1. This person had to be a private in the army. — con man
2. This person said, "You must do everything I say." — president
3. This person marched and marched and marched. — con man

Compound words, copying sentences, characterization

LESSON 60

Name _____

Part 1
Cross out the words that don't have **ar**.

chair	alarm	about	drain	started	talking
army	scream	darted	charge	track	sharp

(crossed out: chair, alarm, about, drain, started, talking, scream, track)

Part 2
Write the name of the person each sentence tells about.

president   **con man**

1. This person said, "I need something to eat." _____ president
2. This person ordered a big lunch for two. _____ con man
3. This person said, "I must get away from this guy." _____ con man
4. This person rolled right off the side of the bed. _____ president
5. This person said, "Just charge it to the room." _____ president
6. This person smiled and said, "Tee, hee." _____ con man

Part 3
The words in the first column have endings. Write the same words without endings in the second column.

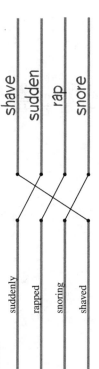

suddenly ——— shave
rapped ——— sudden
snoring ——— rap
shaved ——— snore

LESSON 59

Name _____

Part 1
Write the words.

near	+	by	=	_____ nearby
with	+	out	=	_____ without
be	+	cause	=	_____ because
loud	+	ly	=	_____ loudly

Part 2
Write **1, 2,** or **3** in front of each sentence to show when these things happened in the story. Then write the sentences in the blanks.

3 The president said very loudly, "We are from the bug company."

2 The woman in the main office said, "Take the green car in front of the office."

1 The con man and the president dressed in white jackets and left the shack.

1. The con man and the president dressed in white jackets and left the shack.

2. The woman in the main office said, "Take the green car in front of the office."

3. The president said very loudly, "We are from the bug company."

Part 3
The words in the first column have endings. Write the same words without endings in the second column.

steered ——— stare
nearest ——— near
stared ——— steer

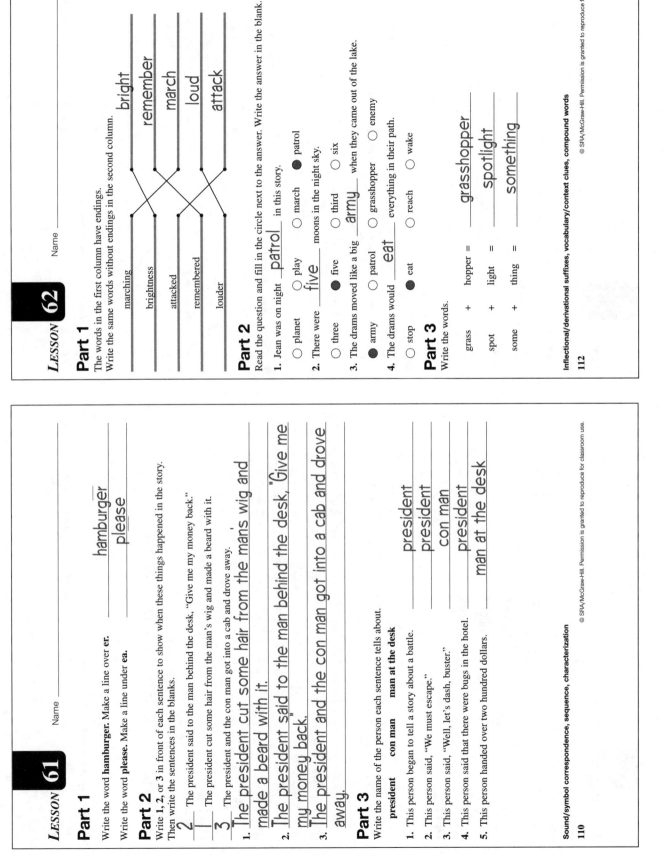

LESSON 61

Name ___

Part 1

Write the word **hamburger.** Make a line over **er.**

hamburger

Write the word **please.** Make a line under **ea.**

please

Part 2

Write **1, 2,** or **3** in front of each sentence to show when these things happened in the story.
Then write the sentences in the blanks.

2 The president said to the man behind the desk, "Give me my money back."

1 The president cut some hair from the man's wig and made a beard with it.

3 The president and the con man got into a cab and drove away.

1. The president cut some hair from the mans wig and
made a beard with it.

2. The president said to the man behind the desk, "Give me
my money back."

3. The president and the con man got into a cab and drove
away.

Part 3

Write the name of the person each sentence tells about.

president   con man   man at the desk

1. This person began to tell a story about a battle.   president

2. This person said, "We must escape."   president

3. This person said, "Well, let's dash, buster."   con man

4. This person said that there were bugs in the hotel.   president

5. This person handed over two hundred dollars.   man at the desk

Sound/symbol correspondence, sequence, characterization

110

© SRA/McGraw-Hill. Permission is granted to reproduce for classroom use.

LESSON 62

Name ___

Part 1

The words in the first column have endings.
Write the same words without endings in the second column.

marching   bright

brightness   remember

attacked   march

remembered   loud

louder   attack

Part 2

Read the question and fill in the circle next to the answer. Write the answer in the blank.

1. Jean was on night ___patrol___ in this story.
   ○ planet   ○ play   ○ march   ● patrol

2. There were ___five___ moons in the night sky.
   ○ three   ● five   ○ third   ○ six

3. The drams moved like a big ___army___ when they came out of the lake.
   ● army   ○ patrol   ○ grasshopper   ○ enemy

4. The drams would ___eat___ everything in their path.
   ○ stop   ● eat   ○ reach   ○ wake

Part 3

Write the words.

grass   +   hopper   =   grasshopper

spot   +   light   =   spotlight

some   +   thing   =   something

Inflectional/derivational suffixes, vocabulary/context clues, compound words

112

© SRA/McGraw-Hill. Permission is granted to reproduce for classroom use.

152

LESSON 63

Name _____

Part 1

Write the words.

her	+	self	=	herself
what	+	ever	=	whatever
moon	+	light	=	moonlight
some	+	body	=	somebody

Part 2

Read the words in the box. Then fill in the blanks.

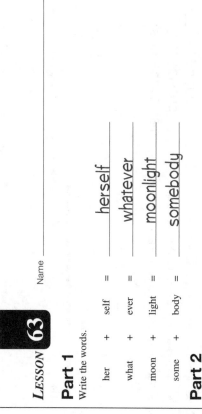

reached	far	shirt	closer	light	signaler
skipped	inches	drams	pocket	pressed	springs
frozen	barracks	messed	meters	melted	stabbed

Jean couldn't seem to move. She stared at the drams as they came __closer__. They were only a few __meters__ from her now.

"Move," she said to herself. But her legs felt as if they had __melted__.

Then Jean began to think. She __reached__ for her __signaler__. She __pressed__ the button. Lights began to flash in the __barracks__. Women began to yell, "The drams! The drams! Let's get out of here."

And Jean began to run. Now her legs felt like __springs__. Did she ever run!

Part 3

Copy the sentence.

Suddenly, a sound came from the other room.

__Suddenly, a sound came from the other room.__

Compound words, vocabulary/context clues, copying sentences

114

LESSON 64

Name _____

Part 1

The words in the first column have endings.
Write the same words without endings in the second column.

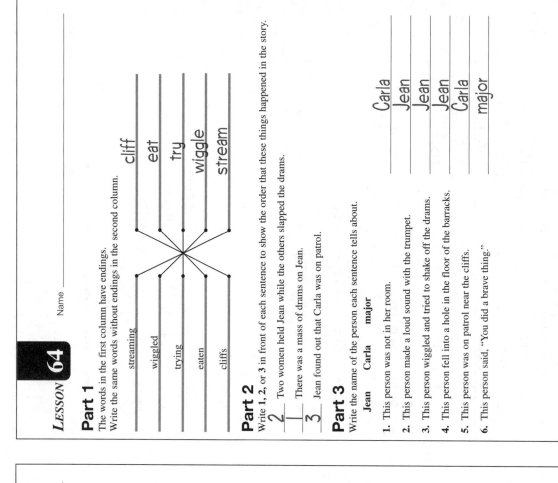

streaming	cliff
wiggled	eat
trying	try
eaten	wiggle
cliffs	stream

Part 2

Write 1, 2, or 3 in front of each sentence to show the order that these things happened in the story.

__2__ Two women held Jean while the others slapped the drams.

__1__ There was a mass of drams on Jean.

__3__ Jean found out that Carla was on patrol.

Part 3

Write the name of the person each sentence tells about.

Jean   Carla   major

1. This person was not in her room. ___Carla___
2. This person made a loud sound with the trumpet. ___Jean___
3. This person wiggled and tried to shake off the drams. ___Jean___
4. This person fell into a hole in the floor of the barracks. ___Jean___
5. This person was on patrol near the cliffs. ___Carla___
6. This person said, "You did a brave thing." ___major___

Inflectional suffixes, sequence, characterization

116

LESSON **65**

Name _____

Part 1

Write **1**, **2**, or **3** in front of each sentence to show the order that these things happened in the story.

___1___ Jean tried to think of everthing that happened just before the drams went to sleep.

___3___ The major told the others why the trumpet made the drams sleep.

___2___ Jean gave a blast on Carla's trumpet.

Part 2

The words in the first column have endings.
Write the same words without endings in the second column.

deeply ————————————— bit

lined ————————————— deep

blushing ————————————— line

bitten ————————————— blush

Part 3

Read the words in the box. Then fill in the blanks.

barracks	bubbles	blushed	sound	fill	smiled
animals	horns	hunger	felt	showed	leave
line	march	patrol	water	hungry	blast

One of the women said, "Does that mean that we can stop the drams just by blowing

__horns__ when they come out of the __water__ ?"

"We can do better than that," the major said. "We can pipe __sound__ into the lake. We can

keep them from getting __hungry__ for sound. Then they won't __leave__ the lake."

The women __smiled__ and looked at each other. Jean was thinking, "Now night

__patrol__ won't be so bad."

Sequence, vocabulary/context clues

118

© SRA/McGraw-Hill. Permission is granted to reproduce for classroom use.

153